TABLE OF CONTENTS

PART I — ACTION

PART II — RESEARCH

APPENDICES

GLOSSARY

The following explanations are presented to clarify the meaning of terms used in this study and are not intended to be technical, dictionary-type definitions.

Action program.	An endeavor in which participants try new practices with the idea of determining whether they work.
Alliance of Schools.	A cooperative association of local schools, districts, Colgate University, BOCES, Che-Mad-Her-On, the State Education Department and other educational institutions for the purpose of pooling their resources to attack the problem of modernization of education.
Analysis of Variance.	The name given to the rationale for the F test process (see F test below).
Articulation.	Coordination between the curricula and/or staff across educational levels, such as high school and university.
Attitude (toward Innovation).	The extent to which school personnel are favorable or unfavorable toward innovation. One of the major criteria in this study. (See Chapter 6.)
Availability.	The extent to which curricular, technological, structural or other innovations are available for teachers to use in a school. One of the major criteria in this study. (See Chapter 6.)
BOCES	The Board of Cooperative Educational Services, a one- to three- county regional board of education and part of the legal structure provided by New York State Educational law to finance school services and practices in two or more local school districts.
Che-Mad-Her-On.	The regional supplementary educational center inaugurated with Federal funds in early 1968 for the purpose of helping local schools and other community educational institutions plan for change or coordinate their efforts to modernize. Its name comes from a combination of the first letters of the four counties which it serves (Chenango, Madison, Herkimer and Oneida). The original proposal for its inauguration came from BOCES and the Kettering-Colgate Project, and from governmental agencies.
Chi Square.	An index showing the extent to which two variables (classified in categories rather than in measured units) are related.
Correlation Coefficient.	An index ranging from zero to + 1.0, showing the degree to which two variables are related. For example, a coefficient of 1.0 indicates that

A STUDY OF INNOVATION AND CHANGE IN EDUCATION

THE REGIONAL UNIVERSITY-SCHOOLS

RESEARCH AND DEVELOPMENT PROGRAM

AN ACTION-RESEARCH PROJECT

Supported By

THE CHARLES F. KETTERING FOUNDATION

and

COLGATE UNIVERSITY

1967 - 1971

ISBN 0-912566-01-9
Library of Congress Card Number 70-166212
Printed in United States of America

George E. Schlesser, Project Director
Robert J. Crowley, Assistant Director of Research
David M. Jenkins, Media Specialist
Mrs. Jennie L. Baumbach, Resource Teacher in English
William J. Moynihan, Resource Teacher in Social Studies
Donald J. Rudy, Resource Teacher

PREFACE

During the past decade, interest in educational change for effective learning has increased sharply. Acceleration began in 1958 with the launching of special programs for the gifted as well as new curricula in sciences, modern languages and mathematics. Federal and state programs were instituted to bring teachers up-to-date in knowledge of their fields, as well as to familiarize them with the new curricula. Academic year and summer institutes and workshops were subsidized. New programs for the disadvantaged were organized.

Private foundations entered the struggle by encouraging new programs in teacher preparation and the studies of educational change. As a specific example of the latter, the Charles F. Kettering Foundation, formerly devoted in the 1960's to biological and cancer research, began allocating part of its energies to the equally challenging problem of educational research. In connection with its interest in educational change, it began sponsoring the Educational section of the *Saturday Review,* which was devoted to narrative accounts of new frontiers in education.

In 1964 and 1965, giant industries, especially those formed through merger of electronic and publishing companies, advanced the premise that technology could change education.

Soon afterward, the hypothesis was advanced that new technologies and curricula would become passing fancies if introduced piecemeal and without adequate accountability based on research and evaluation studies. As a result, some groups placed emphasis on restructuring the whole school. This massive attack by institutions and individuals raised as many problems as it solved. Many teachers with favorable attitudes toward change were being frustrated by school and community conditions that impeded their efforts. Modernization was advancing more rapidly in some schools than in others. Why?

It was during this period, 1966, that the present study was conceived. It addressed itself to the designing of a program that would provide the optimum conditions necessary in which schools and the University and other agencies would be encouraged to try new practices, could study their quality through research and evaluation, and in which creative, innovating teachers would be supported rather than frustrated. The basic procedure was quite simple. Innovations were introduced as effectively as possible in twenty-six schools, and the impact on the schools, the community and regional agencies studied. In a real sense, the action and evaluation phases of the project might be thought of as a process during which a regional model was being designed. Could a regional program be designed that would provide the optimum social conditions and educational support in which teachers and schools tried new practices and determined which ones were most effective? "Optimum conditions" implies greater understanding of the educational climate in both school and community. Knowing whether new practices are effective implies evaluation and research. It is to this question that the study addressed itself.

The report is divided into two sections, action and research. The first section traces the way the Kettering-Colgate Project was planned and operated from the time that individual innovating teachers introduced new practices (1967) through the time the regional model (now called the Alliance of Schools and Colgate University) was conceived. The second section, research, presents findings on the forces at work in the schools and community. It is possible that some of the findings may be generalized to include models for change in higher education or at other levels, although the study was conducted with a focus on secondary

i

education. For example, most institutions face the question of how to bring about effective change. The need to prevent staff obsolescence and provincialism and to foster a problem solving and creative outlook is not unusual among educational as well as other institutions. It may be that such designs as the "ripple approach" and the "peer support" concept discussed in this study are applicable on a broader scale. If so, they are worthy of study over a wider range of fields. To some, the appendices will be as important as the main body, especially to school personnel closely involved in implementing and evaluating new practices.

Major acknowledgment should be made to the Charles F. Kettering Foundation for sponsoring this project, to the twenty-six schools and other cooperating agencies such as the Board of Cooperative Educational Services and Che-Mad-Her-On (the four-county planning center) who worked diligently to make it a success, and to the University officials who provided educational support, encouragement and facilities. For the Foundation, Mr. E.H. Vause was responsible for understanding the potentiality and providing the impetus needed to launch the project. In 1971, visitations by Mr. William Shaw and Mr. Charles Willis were very helpful. It is impossible to acknowledge the assistance of all of those responsible for making this volume possible. The names of the Innovating Teachers appear with the descriptions of their projects in Appendix C. Names of school and other administrators, liaison representatives, project staff members, early planners and involved State Education Department officials appear in Appendix F.

Not all of the available materials have been published in this volume. Interested researchers may wish to write for more technical material, basic data, or other information. Other school personnel may wish more information on the action phase.

G.E.S.

all individuals who rate high on the first variable rate high on the second variable, and all low on the first are low on the second. The index is also commonly used to show the reliability of a measure, or the extent to which an individual will be shown as having the same standing on a retest. It is also used for validity coefficients which check the degree to which an instrument measures what it is purported to measure. The latter is usually some objective outside criterion.

Criterion.
The object or goal of a given project. Usually used in connection with the "measurement of the criterion" or goal for the purpose of determining whether the practice has been successful.

Departmental Unit.
A team of teachers, departmental heads and University consultants organized to study and introduce new practices throughout an entire department of a school. The next step after the "ripple" approach, in which one teacher innovates.

Design.
Refers to a research or action design, which is a plan outlining or diagramming in abstract form the procedure to be followed.

F Test of Significance.
An index showing the extent to which there is a significant difference (beyond chance) between two or more means or other statistics. The test is named after Fisher, a British statistician. If the F is above a given level, the variable being studied can be said to have a significant influence.

Feedback.
Information or other reaction obtained from the participants in a program, used to evaluate and determine the effectiveness of that program.

Financial Resources.
The amount of money perceived to be available for innovations by board members, parents, or others.

Forces (Community and School).
External or internal influences being exerted on the school or within the school.

Innovations.
New educational practices including those in the curriculum (such as in mathematics), technology (such as learning centers) and structure (such as team-teaching or flexible scheduling).

In-Service Training.
Educational programs providing consultant services, conferences, workshops, courses, or other opportunities for experienced teachers to keep up-to-date.

Institutionalization.
A sociological term referring to the tendency of

	a relatively new practice to become an accepted part of the institution's practice and the recipient of financial support through legal channels.
Kettering-Colgate Project.	A three-year action-research project supported by the Charles F. Kettering Foundation and Colgate University in cooperation with twenty-six school districts and regional Boards of Education, and the regional supplementary educational center, for the purpose of influencing change, studying the process at work, and institutionalizing a long-range regional program.
Liaison Representative.	A voluntary staff member in one of the cooperating schools, whose main duties were to coordinate the dispensing and collecting of research bulletins and other information, such as survey instruments in the cooperating schools.
Micro-Teaching.	Practice in teaching a small group of pupils, usually four to nine, under supervision and usually in a televised situation, so that the practicing teacher can later observe himself and discuss changes with the supervisor, or others.
Model.	Refers to a theoretical model or "map" of an "ideal" plan or structure under which new practices can be introduced most effectively. It normally includes statements about: objectives, program, agencies involved, financing, participants and all other interrelated elements necessary for the success of the endeavor. A model may be program oriented or mathematically oriented.
Modernization.	The extent to which a school is up-to-date, or uses new practices.
Organizational Model.	A statement or plan describing the responsibilities of the participating agencies who provide legal, financial or leadership support for a program.
Peer Intervention Strategy.	Socialization or approval and psychological support provided by a large peer group of the staff members from several schools, all of whom view innovation as the normal practice and who tend to resist pressures for return to the habitual practices.
r.	See correlation coefficient.
Research Program.	The evaluation phase of a total program to introduce educational changes. Its purpose is to gather objective information to determine whether the program has been successful. It

	includes a careful study of the objectives of the program, constructing reliable and valid measures of those objectives, and creating designs appropriate to the study.
Resource Teachers.	Staff members associated with the Kettering-Colgate Project, trained as consultants, during the action phase, to the thirty-one innovating teachers for the purpose of assuring the *effective* introduction of innovations into the schools.
Restructuring or Redesign.	Contrasted to the "ripple" approach, the whole school program is studied and plans for changing it are made at the outset.
Ripple Approach (or Effect).	The introduction of one or two new practices into a school, accompanied by an attempt to spread the practice or the concept of innovation to others. The analogy is to the pebble dropped into a quiet pool of water.
Study Councils.	Associations of school administrators and the University, meeting regularly to study and discuss new ideas and plans.
t Test of Significance.	An index showing the extent to which there is a significant difference (beyond chance) between two means or other statistics. Similar to the F Test except that only two means are involved.
Teacher Leadership Development.	The education of prospective and experienced teachers so that they will be up-to-date and capable of being leaders rather than impeders of effective educational change.
Team Teaching.	Distinguished from the usual self-contained classroom in which one teacher is responsible for a group of fifteen to fifty students. A group of teachers together plan the instruction for a large group of students and teach their specialty to large and small groups of students for short or long daily periods, depending on which is most favorable to learning.
Usage.	The extent to which curricular, technological and structural innovations are used by the teachers in a school. One of the major criteria in this study. (See Chapter 6.)
Variables.	Attributes or other elements measured to provide a range or the distribution in standings among individuals or institutions, so that one attribute may be correlated or compared to others to show whether it makes an important contribution to the study, and whether it has significant relationships to other attributes.

Figures

Exhibits

CHAPTER 1
INTRODUCTION

Because education is of vital importance to all men, its reformation is a crucial problem today and has been over the ages. Changing the schools, an essential phase of man's education, is a major subject of debate by reformers from all walks of life. There is little need to document this statement by listing names, including submarine experts, philosophers, media editors, politicians, as well as educators. Their names are legion. The main point is that those of us who want to bring about constructive change need to understand the forces at work, both positive and negative.

A study of many of these forces, both internal and external to the school, is the aim of this project. Forces within the school include those exerted by administrators, teachers and pupils, and the organizational climate in which they work. Forces from outside the school include those exerted by school board members, parents and others in the region. For purposes of research, this study has not included such external agencies as foundations and national associations. The focus has been on the process of change in the unit where change takes place; namely in the local schools. The contention is:

1. that constructive change can be brought about by a combination of action and research at the regional level; and
2. that study of what happens when innovations are effectively and cooperatively introduced can result in an understanding of the forces at work.

One of the great shortcomings of action attempts today is that by trying to arouse people to the need for change, they wind up convincing people that education is in a sorry shape. This gives opponents of education, per se, a chance to "move in" to cut funds, and to strike telling blows at the teaching profession through legislation. Other disenchanted persons may be led to inaugurate new endeavors outside of the establishment. Usually their efforts have little lasting impact, but the oscillations they produce are damaging to the quality of education. It is our contention that action objectives can be achieved best through regional cooperation and the designing of models which call for the use of resources of a local region and make full use of legally constituted agencies. If these agencies are inadequate, legal machinery exists to correct the needed administrative unit.

Currently, one of the shortcomings of research and evaluation, a second aspect of the problem, is the lack of genuine interest in evidence as to the success of new practices. The consequences of such indifference are lack of continuity of research, shortage of valid and reliable evaluation instruments and improper attention to design. One explanation is that we are so busy operating the programs and writing proposals for new ones that there is little time left for "pure research," building instruments, and for reading the research findings of others.

In our action research program, conducted in conjunction with secondary schools of the region, the major *research* objective has been to determine the impact and influence of the effective introduction of selected innovations on actual change and on change in attitudes of various publics. The major *action* objective has been to build a cooperative organization which would give support and continuity to the Regional College-Schools Research and Development Program. This emerged as an organization of selected school districts, the University, and other agencies working together to influence educational change directly in the region and indirectly in the nation.

1

This report is divided into two major sections:

1. the action section, in which the organizational model for the region is discussed; and
2. the research and evaluation section in which findings with respect to school and community forces are presented.

The former will be useful to educational institutions and agencies contemplating the launching of educational redesign projects of lasting impact and may serve as a guide or model to those who wish to work within existing legal agencies.

The second will help practitioners by providing leads and theory about forces that need to be harnessed. It will also help by furnishing research instruments, procedures and designs for the evaluation of their projects. It is hoped that the total report will be useful in improving the processes of action and research.

The action section which follows is divided into two parts:

1. the action plan of the immediate Kettering-Colgate Project, which was launched to study the potentialities for building an overall organizational structure; and
2. the overall organizational model itself.

Critical Issues

Several critical issues will appear as this report progresses. They will be listed here for emphasis:

1. Operational Plan: in designing a regional program for implementing change, how should the operating plan be arranged? Should a school be isolated from its district or considered a part of it? Is the school building and staff the unit in which change takes place?
2. Overall Legal Structure: can the relevant educational institutions in a region form a long-range Alliance to bring about effective change in goals and procedures? The beginning of such an Alliance has been one of the results of the Kettering-Colgate Project. In an Alliance, the resources of educational institutions in the region are utilized to bring about effective change in aims, curriculum, technology and structure.

   Should a project work separately from the existing framework of control so as to conduct research and implement action, uninhibited by the impeding forces of the establishment? Or should a project work with the administrative units of existing organizations with the aim of institutionalizing the results of the project so that the changes will continue after the innovation is completed? It will be seen that the Kettering-Colgate Project used the latter approach, allying itself with the administration and school board, Board of Cooperative Educational Services, Colgate University, Che-Mad-Her-On, and the State Education Department. This is in contrast to other current projects, such as privately sponsored teacher accountability assessments.
3. The Ripple Approach vs. Restructuring: what approach should be used in introducing innovations to bring about effective change? Is restructuring the school more effective than the "ripple effect" of introducing one or two innovations in each school and providing for dissemination? What are the advantages and disadvantages of each, and which results in more effective long-range change? For example, the New York State Education Department has selected four model school systems as redesign schools, with the intent of involving the community in selecting educational alternatives. In contrast, the

2

Kettering-Colgate Project used the "ripple approach" in its initial phase. To provide the "ripple" the innovating teacher in each of the twenty-six schools effectively introduced an innovation and actively attempted to diffuse it and his enthusiasm for change to other staff members in the school and to school board members and parents. (See Chapter 5.)

4. The Process of Change: what theory of educational change should a project adopt with respect to these questions:
   a. What changes are most important? Should emphasis be on:
      1. values,
      2. curriculum, or
      3. technology?
   b. What are the key influence groups in the school:
      1. the administration,
      2. the faculty and administration working as a team, or
      3. the faculty?
   c. What are the other key influence groups:
      1. board members,
      2. parents,
      3. students, or
      4. professional associations?
   d. Can a project start with technological innovations and progress to values? Can a project begin with the "ripple approach" and progress to re-structuring? How a project decides these issues will determine the scope of its activities and the nature of the instruments with which it will evaluate results.

5. Evaluation: can endeavors to bring about change be systematically evaluated by studying effects? If so, how? What effects should be evaluated and for whom: pupils, staff, board members, parents, or taxpayers? Can hard evidence be gathered? The instruments selected and prepared by the Project are a step in this direction and may be of interest to other regions.

6. Design of Innovations: who designs the innovations to be introduced in the experimental schools? What are sources of innovative ideas?

7. Teacher Preparation: should students preparing to teach (interns and student teachers) be a part of the project? If not, how can they learn modern practices? Must all beginning teachers be re-tooled?

8. Articulation: will regional projects lead to great coordination between school and University, with respect to teacher preparation and in-service programs? Will school and University faculty be interchanged more? Will the sharp distinction be removed between secondary school and University for some students, and more student exchange result? Will it lead to greater involvement of parents and others in planning? As schools, universities, and communities work together more closely, several new ways of pooling their resources to attack common problems such as the above, may appear.

9. Influences on the University: will such an innovative project improve the University facilities and benefit its faculty and students?

10. Planning for Change: will an understanding of the forces facilitating and impeding change lead to more effective planning and implementation? The next step after the "ripple approach" may be broad planning by all concerned: parents, board members, administrators, teachers, Boards of Cooperative Educational Services, Che-Mad-Her-On, the University and the State Education

3

Department. Will cooperative planning institutionalize the effective changes, so that they and the Alliance can have long-range support? These and other issues will be discussed as our report progresses.

The Colgate University Campus in a rural setting.

Part 1
ACTION

Schools differed — Two buildings

CHAPTER 2
THE ACTION DESIGN FOR EFFECTIVE CHANGE: 1968 - 1969

How should change be initiated? Some writers argue that, to be effective, a plan for change should encompass the total school program. Furthermore, they claim that those plans directed at the instructional program and utilization of media tend to be characterized by disjointedness and seem to influence administrative efficiency, rather than improve the teaching-learning process. They imply that changing the school as a whole should be the first step.

The Kettering-Colgate Project took a contrary view; namely, that there were many individual teachers ready to innovate, even though the school was not, and that by effectively introducing innovations, the spirit and know-how of individual teachers would be diffused; first to the departmental unit, and then throughout the school. The phrase "effective introduction" meant that the teachers needed to be retooled. This was done by resource teachers and consultants. Materials and equipment were developed or provided. The project discovered, however, that single innovating projects were only a first step toward total school involvement. It soon progressed from using the single innovating teacher to involving a whole department in a school as the change agent. How the operational plan unfolded, is the story of this chapter. Figure II-1 graphically illustrates this plan as it progressed.

Perhaps the question comes to this: "If you were the responsible head of a foundation, governmental agency project, or school, where would you invest your limited funds — in a 'ripple' or restructuring type of action program?"

During the first year, twenty-six experimental schools were selected in a five-county region surrounding the University. All of these schools were public secondary schools and varied from large urban high schools to small rural central schools. The initial criteria for selection was a willingness of the schools to participate in the study. After the schools were selected, pre-measures of the various populations were obtained.

The action phase, the second year of the project, began with the call for proposals from the experimental schools. The project looked for innovative proposals in the areas of English, social studies, mathematics, science, and administrative procedures. Its definition of innovation was "a practice that was new to that particular school, but not necessarily to education as a whole." In most cases, these proposals came from individual teachers, although several groups of teachers submitted proposals, as did several administrators. The proposals were screened, and final selection was based upon the quality of the proposal, administrative support, qualifications of the prospective innovator and ability of the project to finance and support the innovation.

Thirty-one innovations were selected and implemented in the twenty-six* experimental schools. These were funded in whole or in part by the Project. They were in four subject fields and quite varied in nature, as shown in Exhibit II-1. (See Appendix C for full descriptions.) Innovators were given a free hand in ordering materials, up to budget restrictions, to implement the innovations.

Five resource teachers were employed for one year to work on a consulting basis with the various innovators. During the summer of 1968, the selected innovators attended an individualized training session at the University. Topics

*One additional school entered the project for which data were not complete.

5

covered included operation of audio-visual equipment, production of teaching materials, effective design, utilization of media, and curriculum design. These sessions were also used to familiarize the resource teachers with the school projects, and help innovators design and select the educational materials.

EXHIBIT II-1. LIST OF INNOVATIVE PROJECTS CONDUCTED IN THE EXPERIMENTAL SCHOOLS

Social Science
1. Large-group small-group Instruction Using the Fenton Inquiry Approach (10)
2. Innovative Instruction for Race Relations in America (12)
3. Individual Instruction for the Slow Learner (9)
4. The Closed Circuit T.V. in Social Studies (7)
5. Multi-Media Approach to Social Studies (7)
6. Teacher Improvement through Inter-Action Analysis (7-12)

Science
7. Harvard Project Physics (11 and 12)
8. Portable Closed Circuit T.V. for Science Instruction
9. The Portable Closed Circuit T.V. in Junior High Science (7-9)
10. Experimental Earth Science Curriculum (ESP) (9-12)
11. Portable Closed Circuit T.V. in Chemistry (11-12)
12. Project Teaching in Advanced Biology
13. Biology Honors Program (12)
14. Use of Videotape in Biology Laboratory (10 and 12)
15. Intensive Study in Advanced Biology (12)

Mathematics
16. Application of an Electronic Calculator (11-12)
17. Application of the Electronic Calculator (11)
18. Uses of the Computer in Class Room Testing (11)
19. Mathematics Curriculum Center (8)
20. Mathematics Resource Center (8)
21. Junior High Mathematics Laboratory (7)

General
22. General Evaluation of Instruction Using Portable T.V. (12)

English
23. Propaganda and the Video Tape in the Speech Class (11)
24. A modified Humanities Course for the Non-college Bound (12)
25. A Composition Approach Using Cassettes (12)
26. Multi-Media for Creative Communication (9-10)
27. Laboratory for Reading (7-9)
28. Using the VTR as a Resource in Speech and Discussion Sessions (11)
29. Self-Improvement through Use of Videotapes (9-12)
30. Writing Clinic Using Tape Recorders (10)
31. Creativity in English for Non-Regents Seniors (12)

During the school years, 1968-1969 and 1969 to May 1970, the action phase of the project was in full swing. Effective implementation of the innovation required a great deal of time and effort on the part of the innovators (see Chapter 5). Also, the resource teachers held weekly conferences with the innovators in their schools.

The need to continue the projects during the third year, the evaluation period, was evident. To cut off help at the end of the action phase (second year) would have been prejudicial to the evaluation, as well as to the long-range goals.

A Springboard for Departmental Units

The innovations initiated during the second year of the Kettering-Colgate Project (1968-69) directly involved only one or two teachers in each school. As the action phase drew to a close, a number of schools expressed a desire to continue working with the University on the programs. Many of these requests involved capitalizing upon work begun by the Kettering-Colgate Project in a coordinated, departmental endeavor within the schools.

The University encouraged the development of this interest because it related directly to the desired objective of diffusion of innovations in project schools. It appeared a natural avenue for the long-range goal of facilitating the development of teaching centers, an original goal of the project, in a few select schools thus serving as models for effective change in the region.

After careful consideration, the decision was made to alter the nature of the teaching center concept. Originally, teaching centers were to be located in four schools of the region and to contain curriculum material, media equipment and programmed reference material. "At these teaching centers the value of innovations was to be demonstrated to teachers in these and other schools." However, a more viable plan became evident as a result of exchange of ideas with the schools. Several disadvantages to the teaching center concept were seen:
1. teachers of other schools could not travel great distances to obtain materials and equipment, thus the main beneficiaries would be the schools in which the center was located;
2. the center idea did not include a procedure for prospective teacher leadership development; and
3. the teaching center concept made no provision for cooperative planning among the schools and the University.

Consequently, a new plan was designed for what was later to be called the Alliance of Schools. It was to be implemented in two steps:
1. the exploration and action stage during 1969-70 and
2. a formal alliance of schools and the University phase (1970-71 and beyond).

Departmental Units for School-University Cooperation (1969-70)

Efforts during the initial phase concentrated on four social studies departments in Norwich, Hamilton, Sherburne-Earlville, and Morrisville-Eaton Central schools. Selection of schools was based upon agreement of individual department members with the goals of the project and past evidence of cooperation with similar undertakings. Administrators and school board agreement to cooperate with the program also formed an important part of the qualifications. Besides agreeing with the short-term planning objectives mentioned above, the departments agreed with the goal of developing informed, decision-making departmental units. Administrators and school boards were expected to show their support for the project by

*Tanner, Daniel - *Secondary Curriculum,* The Macmillan Co., N.Y., 1971, pp. 403-405.

various means, including the granting of inservice credit and the provision of planning and meeting time during the year. The University staff decided to limit the project to the social studies area for the first year simply to conserve and concentrate resources.

After a number of meetings with area teachers, administrators, and school board members, four schools were selected who agreed to cooperate. In an effort to make the project "teacher centered" rather than simply an idea developed by the University, a summer workshop was scheduled for late August for the purpose of planning the activities for the school year. Representatives for this sesssion were chosen by their respective departments. They and the University consultants are listed in Appendix F.

The atmosphere of the one-week August workshop was informal but a tight schedule was followed. A number of areas relating to the project were explored which topically included:

1. Overview of the objectives and philosophy of the Kettering-Schools team approach to innovation
2. Theory of Departmental Unit Organization
3. Preparation and evaluation of behavioral objectives
4. Training on the video tape recorder and other media
5. Planning objectives and programs for meetings to be held at the University for all participants during the year
6. Unstructured time for participants to familiarize themselves with the resources of the University and become personally acquainted with each other and the University staff.

Of prime importance to the participants was the planning of the academic year, action phase of the project. These plans were drawn up but considered only tentative in nature depending upon reactions of other members of the department and feedback from initial undertakings. First, plans were made for activities which would be of value for all four departments in common. Second, plans were considered for activities of each individual department which would take into consideration its own unique school population, resources, and areas of concern. Video tape recorders were provided for schools in an effort to provide an additional means for facilitating communication of ideas among schools, as well as introducing what turned out to be a valuable tool for social studies instruction and teacher development.

As a result of the discussions at the August workshop a series of monthly meetings for all participants was planned. The planning group attempted to make the meetings problem solving and discussion oriented, although several lectures were included. The meetings held at the University were modified as the year continued but centered around the following general areas:

1. Taxonomy of Educational Objectives and their application to social studies
2. Recent trends in social studies
3. The new media and the social studies
4. Flexible scheduling and flexible staff deployment
5. Independent study programs, large group - small group instruction, and intra-class grouping
6. Evaluation and testing
7. Organizational and planning considerations of the group itself for the purpose of facilitating innovation into the future.

The August workshop participants continued to function and meet during the school year for the purposes of evaluating the monthly meetings, further planning of future meetings, exploring new ideas in relation to the project, and providing feedback on the progress and problems of individual departmental units. Administrators cooperated by releasing departmental representatives for this purpose during school time.

While the seminars held at the University attempted to explore common areas of concern, a number of activities were carried out by the individual departments as part of the project. At the request of the teachers, the staff at Colgate became involved in varying degrees in these activities. Some examples of the consultant services conducted with individual departments during the year included: interpretation and application of standardized tests; teacher-generated evaluation techniques; applications to appropriate funding agencies to further departmental objectives; training in use and application of media; equipping and planning the use of a social studies resource room; and, primarily, curriculum redesign work. Such contacts with two of the schools far exceeded those with the other two, possibly due to prior, strong informal relationships established in these between the teachers and University staff.

Evaluative feedback was also provided to the project departments giving them an insight into the functioning of the individual departmental units. An instrument was devised and administered which related to such items as degree of group regulation, cohesiveness, productivity, and initiative. Reactions of participants were also elicited concerning the relevancy of content and mode of presentation of the monthly meetings.

Partial evidence of success of the project was indicated when the group decided to continue to function as a unit into the next school year (1970-71) even though reduction of funds would limit certain services provided by the University. Part of the May meeting at the University was devoted to organizational considerations, and ideas were referred to the planning committee to formalize. The main change was in the direction of greater control of activities by the teachers involved -- a move supported and encouraged by the University staff and, in fact, one of their original goals. The planning committee report reads as follows:

"EXHIBIT II-2. Report of Area Social Studies Project Planning Committee,
Project Status 1970-71

The committee recommends the continuation of the project in modified form for next year. It was felt that the role of the committee should not be to structure activities and content to any great extent, but that the structure should grow out of the smaller group meetings held beginning next year. However, the following limited structures are suggested:

Continue holding meetings at Colgate University;

Divide according to levels taught (i.e., junior high, senior high, grade level when deemed necessary);

Initially concentrate on building curricula and sharing ideas for the slow learner;

Hold large group meetings for lectures, demonstrations, etc., when deemed necessary by small groups;

Invite students in to react to our considerations and to initiate new thinking on our part;

Use more video-tapes in sharing ideas of individual teachers;

Keep number of participants the same for the present time;

Utilize staff at Colgate University in a manner in which they will be involved in the curriculum development projects;

Preview and evaluate new materials such as games, A-V materials and films;

Obtain inservice college credit for work next year in curriculum development;

Place greater emphasis on communication and cooperation between departments (i.e., exchange of teachers between schools for short periods of time, video tapes, time set aside to consider and help with innovative projects being conducted in some departments.)"

Coming out of this pilot project were many participants who were to initiate the Alliance of Schools and University.

Comments

In summary, the four-school departmental unit plan provided the necessary framework of cooperation for the Alliance of Schools and the University, the long-range model.

During the 1968-70 project the following important insights emerged:

1. University-school cooperation is of greater benefit to both types of institutions than expected. One participant, when asked by an observer whether the University was really important to the school, said, "It is absolutely vital. The school faculty would exist in a vacuum were it not for this relationship." Sometimes this is called the support function which is needed simply to provide status to new practices. But it is more than this. It provides resources (material and human) on which neither type of institution has a monopoly.

2. Both the schools and the University have problems which can be better solved cooperatively than separately. Both have problems of teacher leadership development. The experienced teachers desire a new kind of inservice training which is more continuous than that provided by occasional course work. The University wants to prepare more effective beginning teachers and establish optimum conditions in which they can learn. This implies that the inexperienced teacher would become a team member, working with the more experienced. Optimum conditions imply that the staffs of the schools and the University be studying and working together to effectively introduce innovations and change.

3. To implement the plan, a legal organizational structure needs to be arranged to provide support and to assure that the program will last after the Kettering-Colgate Project ceases. It will continue if it becomes institutionalized; namely, if formally approved by the schools, their local boards and regional agencies, as discussed in Chapter 3.

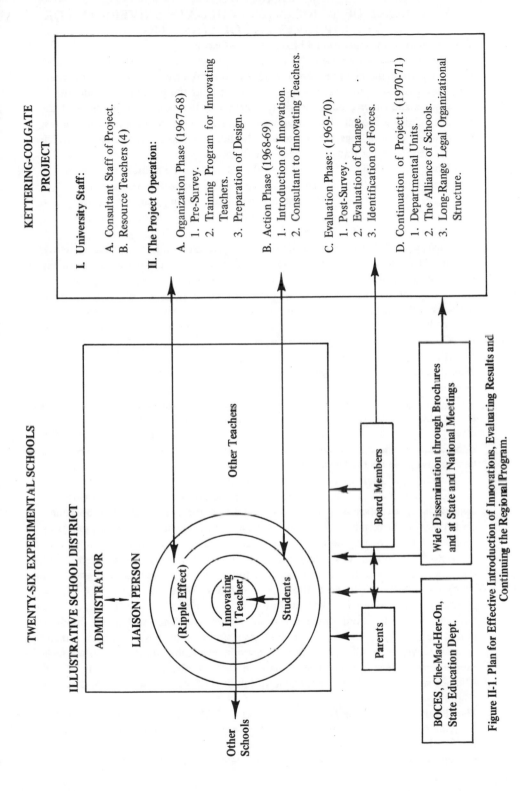

KETTERING-COLGATE PROJECT

I. **University Staff:**
   A. Consultant Staff of Project.
   B. Resource Teachers (4)

II. **The Project Operation:**

   A. Organization Phase (1967-68)
      1. Pre-Survey.
      2. Training Program for Innovating Teachers.
      3. Preparation of Design.

   B. Action Phase (1968-69)
      1. Introduction of Innovation.
      2. Consultant to Innovating Teachers.

   C. Evaluation Phase: (1969-70).
      1. Post-Survey.
      2. Evaluation of Change.
      3. Identification of Forces.

   D. Continuation of Project: (1970-71)
      1. Departmental Units.
      2. The Alliance of Schools.
      3. Long-Range Legal Organizational Structure.

TWENTY-SIX EXPERIMENTAL SCHOOLS

ILLUSTRATIVE SCHOOL DISTRICT

ADMINISTRATOR

LIAISON PERSON

Other Teachers

(Ripple Effect)

Innovating Teacher

Students

Other Schools

Board Members

Parents

Wide Dissemination through Brochures and at State and National Meetings

BOCES, Che-Mad-Her-On, State Education Dept.

Figure II-1. Plan for Effective Introduction of Innovations, Evaluating Results and Continuing the Regional Program.

CHAPTER 3
THE ALLIANCE OF SCHOOLS AND COLGATE UNIVERSITY FOR THE IMPROVEMENT OF EDUCATION

Development of the Operational Phase of the Alliance

The Alliance, as proposed, did not grow full-blown out of a theoretical model. It resulted from the planning sessions and exploratory efforts previously described. Very likely, it could not have been a success without the preliminary endeavor of the schools and other agencies working together in the earlier action phase of the Kettering-Colgate Project. That stage was necessary so that all concerned could test the value of working together and to see whether it was to the self-interests of each party relative to other things that they might do.

What is the Alliance? It might be thought of as the vehicle through which cooperative efforts to bring about change can be supported and encouraged. It recognizes the desirability of pooling resources among schools, between the University, schools and other agencies. Consideration of two of its major features may provide insights into the concept.

First, it establishes the conditions favorable to change. Extra graduate interns, preparing to teach, are added to a school's staff to reduce the teaching load of the experienced teachers so that they have time for implementing change and for supervising the interns. Reduction of load does not explain the dynamics of what happens, but it is essential. Those inside and outside of the schools are coming to realize that teachers and department heads must be provided at least a little time to think and create.

Also, "spin off" features accrue. For example, the beginning teacher (intern) gains understanding and expertise with respect to modern, up-to-date teaching--learning processes. He does not have to be retooled later, because he has not learned in an antiquated system. All concerned are scheduled to make maximum use of their specialties, especially in team-teaching situations. Because interns are directly connected with the University, its resources become available. Because the interns are in the schools under the systematic plan, excellent school resources become available for the University.

Second, the Alliance creates the organization for long-range support for new practices that have proved themselves. Even more important, it provides an organizational structure which encourages and re-enforces a climate of inquiry and creativeness in its member schools. Almost everyone understands that new practices themselves tend to become outmoded. It is the spirit or process of inquiry that needs to be nurtured. As Whitehead said, "Education which is not modern shares the fate of all organic things that are kept too long." What was modern practice a century ago does not fit the critical needs of today. The knowledge explosion, the population explosion and the revolution in communication media are phrases indicating that the word "modernization" is relative. That which was modern practice a century ago is now out-of-date, even though some basic principles remain the same. What the Alliance does is to provide an organizational structure which supports and rewards a creative climate in the schools. The functioning of the Alliance will become clearer as the description of the 1969-70 pilot programs at two schools unfolds.

The Pilot Alliance Program at Sherburne-Earlville Central School (1969-70).

Evolving out of the 1969-70 program (see Chapter 2) came a desire on the part of the Sherburne-Earlville Social Studies Department to continue working with the University on a variety of educational changes (large-group and small-group

12

instruction); increased emphasis on individualized learning; development and effective utilization of a social studies resource center; curriculum revision; and differentiated staff deployment; all directed toward developing curious, creative, self-starting teacher-learners. Furthermore, the department agreed to a bold new step; namely, that development of teacher-leaders, experienced or inexperienced, would be an integral part of the project, in conjunction with the Colgate Intern Program.

To facilitate the changes desired by the social studies department, the University and other cooperating educational agencies agreed to make the following contributions:

1. provide a University consulting team to participate in planning for and experimentation with innovation;
2. provide course work in supervision and curriculum development for department leaders (optional);
3. help in submitting proposals for future funding;
4. make available qualified interns who would assume reduced responsibilities for proportionally reduced salaries (with incomes supplemented by University Intern Scholarships);
5. plan for support of a summer workshop for teachers in the departments and for interns;
6. plan support for equipment and materials needed for the project;
7. continue to coordinate the Sherburne-Earlville department's activities with the on-going project involving the social studies departments in other schools;
8. establish teacher-development teams consisting of two interns a semester, a master teacher, college supervisor, and methods professor; and
9. further develop the Social Studies Resource Center at the University for use of participants (science, mathematics and English were later to have similar centers).

The Sherburne-Earlville Board of Education encouraged the development of this pilot project by increasing financial support to the department for intern salaries, and for planning and meeting time.

Morrisville-Eaton Central School also experimented with a similar but modified model during 1970-71, in preparation for the more full-scale initiation in 1971-72. Although emphasis was on social studies departments during 1969-70 and for pilot programs in 1970-71 in Sherburne-Earlville and Morrisville-Eaton, the Alliance plan calls for inclusion of other departments in 1972-73, depending upon the wishes of the school involved and the resources of the University.

The Plan for 1971-72. Individual departments within schools, in cooperation with other departments in the Alliance and the University, plan to study and implement new curricula and new approaches, including media, staffing, and scheduling changes. They have agreed that an integral part of the project should include the development of teacher-leaders in conjunction with the Colgate University Intern Program, whose interns are expected to become more deeply aware of the process of educational change through observation, participation and research.

The University is to provide curriculum consultants; research and evaluation advice; communication, using the network established by the Kettering-Colgate Project; and help in the coordination of inter-district endeavors. A portion of staff load is allocated to allow active participation in school departmental activities and inter-district seminars. Highly able interns are recruited and through micro-teaching and other activities, are prepared to teach prior to being assigned to schools.

13

Resources of the University, including the self-instructional media center and materials from the Resource Center are made available to all participants. Research and evaluation is part of the process.

The plan for the Alliance initially called for the participation of five schools in 1971-72, with the number of teachers and departments in each school depending upon outside funding. Teachers and administrators from all five schools had been actively involved in developing the plan and had been participants in the activities stimulated over the past three years. Outside funding was not received, so the number of schools has been reduced to two or three for 1971-72 and support sought from internal sources (the local schools, the University, and Boards of Cooperative Educational Services).

Summary. For the schools, the Alliance means working for change through a variety of means, including workshops; inservice training programs; the introduction of curricular, staffing, scheduling and technological innovations; regional cooperation with other schools and the University; and the increased professionalization of the teaching staff. For the University, it requires a type of leadership and participation that has often been missing in the educational history of the country. It requires articulation among the staffs and participation by teachers and administrators in the development of teacher-leaders, able to cope with, and indeed, initiate change leading to the improvement of instruction and learning.

Included in the plan are:

1. model unit teams of school and University staff which are professional, functional, and decision-making units in several Alliance schools to bring about the effective introduction of innovations; and
2. provisions whereby interns and undergraduate practice teachers actively participate with these departmental units in the change process, using the concept of differentiated staffing and new roles for the team members, of which the interns are a part.

The Supporting Organizational Structure

One of the problems facing all innovative projects supported by grants is the question of whether the change will continue after the special funds are no longer available. Many times innovations die because they have not been an integral part of the basic organizational structure. From the time of inception they may have been something "in addition" to the existing program and not a part of it. When the extra support is withdrawn, the schools find it necessary to discontinue the project. The needed support may be either financial or organizational or both.

There are several possible organizational models:

1. The model may have three elements consisting of selected schools (single buildings in a district), the University, and a foundation or agency which supports the project. The project may provide information to the other elements, such as the larger school district, the county or regional Board of Education, and the State Education Department, but may not be considered an integral part of the structure. In this design the foundation project is the key control unit.
2. The State Education Department may be the key influence. It is instrumental in selecting a limited number of schools for re-design. It convinces each school administrator of the value of the innovation, and provides financial and consultant services. Administrators reorganize their schools to inaugurate the redesign plan. It may by-pass regional Boards of Education Services, the regional supplementary educational center, and the universities, but may encourage local planning with parents and board members.

14

3. The third model is the one employed in this project. Hopefully, it shows promise of becoming part of the total existing educational structure. In this region in New York State there are six organizational elements which have been involved in the plan (The Alliance of Schools). These are: the local schools, Boards of Education, Boards of Cooperative Education Services (BOCES), Che-Mad-Her-On, the New York State Education Department, and the University.

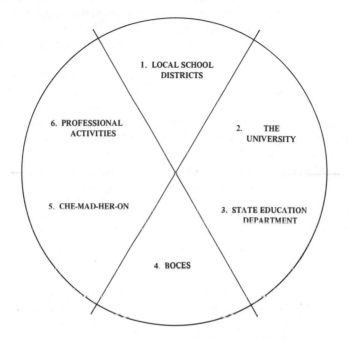

1. LOCAL SCHOOL DISTRICTS
1. The Administration and Departmental Units are the Innovators.
2. Initiates the request for the Alliance Program.

2. THE UNIVERSITY
1. The Department of Education serves a consulting leadership role in the Alliance.
2. Provides interns and student teachers.
3. Provides resources such as media and curriculum centers and consultants.

3. STATE EDUCATION DEPARTMENT
1. Responsible for quality education in the State.
2. Approves new BOCES programs such as the Alliance and Che-Mad-Her-On.
3. Develops State-wide master plans.

4. BOCES
1. The administrative unit for the Alliance.
2. Provides a means for obtaining State aid for the improvement of instruction and teacher leadership development.

5. CHE-MAD-HER-ON
1. The supplementary educational center.
2. Assists school districts and other educational institutions in cooperative planning for redesign.

6. PROFESSIONAL ACTIVITIES
1. They are becoming increasingly responsible for the improvement of instruction and the quality of their personnel.
2. Can be a strong force in approving or rejecting the intern plan and particular programs for the improvement of instruction.

Figure. III-1.   A Model Showing the Supporting Organizational Structure for the Alliance

Figure III-1 is an abbreviated diagram of the proposed supporting organizational structure for the Alliance. It shows seven elements and lists their major roles. A narrative description of these roles is provided in the discussion that follows.

Board of Cooperative Educational Services. The largest administrative units in the region are the Boards of Cooperative Educational Services. These regional boards were inaugurated several decades ago for the purpose of providing shared services (shared teachers) to small schools which could not afford to hire full-time teachers for subjects in which there were small enrollments. Since that time, the definition of "shared services" has been enlarged so that it includes shared programs in which local school districts, working together, are able to offer programs that no single school could provide (e.g., the program for occupational education). The State Education Department provides state-aid at the same rate as for local school districts (often as high as 85 percent). In this it receives help from federal sources, especially for the occupational school and programs for the handicapped or disadvantaged. The concept of the school service is now expanding to include the area of concern of this study; namely, programs for the improvement of instruction and teacher-leadership development. The regional concept for support of cooperative programs is growing.

In 1969-70 the Madison Oneida County BOCES, as a way of showing cooperation with the Kettering-Colgate Project, set aside a small sum to encourage schools to submit proposals for the improvement of instruction. Among the proposals approved, was the Morrisville-Eaton school project. This provided the impetus for the Delaware-Chenango-Otsego Board of Cooperative Educational Services to do the same for Sherburne-Earlville, Greene and Oxford in 1970-71 and laid the groundwork for BOCES approval of the Alliance of Schools plan for 1971-72.

For 1971-72 local Boards of Education have submitted a proposal and a budget to the Madison-Oneida BOCES, the administrative unit for the Alliance. BOCES will seek approval from the State Education Department. If approved, the program will have taken a first step toward becoming institutionalized because it then becomes a part of the legally constituted structure and not dependent upon short-time grant funds.

The Local School District. Of primary importance, of course, is the individual school in which the Alliance is to function. To be accepted, a plan such as the Alliance of Schools needs to be of vital importance to the faculty and administration. Local schools and school boards have many programs competing for funds and only the most important receive sufficient endorsement by administrators and boards to be recommended to BOCES. The local school district is the key element. BOCES cannot initiate a program unless it is requested by two or more schools. Fundamentally then, the initiative must come from the School District and its Board of Education.

With good reason, the Kettering-Colgate Project placed the initiative in the schools. Schools chose their own innovations, and in many other ways were directly responsible for future growth of the program. University consultants worked with teachers and administrators as colleagues during the 1969-70 departmental-unit phase. By 1971-72, at least two of the school districts were ready to request the services of the Alliance of Schools program from their Boards of Cooperative Educational Services.

The School Board. Later this report will discuss the influence of board members.(Chapter 7). It will tend to disagree with one author who says that the

16

Board of Education is not a strong agent in determining the path of innovation. If a board member has students in school, or if he otherwise is vitally interested in improvements, he is apt to be a large influence on the support of programs such as the Kettering-Colgate Project and the Alliance. Furthermore, approval and support by the Board of Education makes the programs an official policy of the school, and is a first step in establishing the program as a regular part of the system.

Che-Mad-Her-On. This four-county (Chenango, Madison, Herkimer and Oneida Counties) supplementary educational center grew out of efforts of the Madison-Oneida County Board of Cooperative Educational Services and the University, to establish an organization to assist school districts in planning for innovation with the help of Title III funds. It was incorporated in 1967 and has been a close working ally of the Kettering-Colgate Project, which helped to create it.

It has funds only to help in planning and not for implementation. Funds for the Alliance come through a pooling of resources from the Kettering-Colgate Project, the School Districts, the University and BOCES. It currently is helping ten regional schools plan re-design projects. Che-Mad-Her-On is a model for planning that others might wish to follow. Its directors have been of assistance in planning and launching the Alliance of Schools. In recommending the Alliance of Schools to the State Education Department, it said, "Che-Mad-Her-On, our Regional Supplementary Education Center, has been involved in planning the proposal (for the Alliance) since its original inception. We endorse it wholeheartedly and recommend its funding. --- It is an extremely interesting and exciting proposal which has tremendous potential for change."

The State Education Department. The State has an important role in the organizational structure. It approves proposals for shared services (from BOCES). It was influential in the establishment of Che-Mad-Her-On and hopefully will continue to provide support to that Center. Furthermore, through grants to schools and colleges and re-design projects, it helps support local innovations. Its present policy is toward the formation of regional programs, both for the improvement of instruction and for preparation of professional personnel. Thus a program such as the Alliance for Schools may fit with the State's regional plans. It does so with respect to the two aspects of the Alliance; improvement of instruction and intern arrangements.

The University. Colgate University, a liberal arts college, has a long tradition in the preparation of teachers. Its Department of Education was the seventh to be formed in the nation, in 1894. In recent years it has worked cooperatively with regional schools on a number of programs to the benefit of all concerned. A basic question has been how it can work with the schools to build an over-all coordinated program for the effective preparation of teachers and inservice for experienced teachers and other professional personnel. A closely related question is, "How can it work to build teaching conditions of improved quality, so that student teachers, interns and experienced teachers can grow in stature?" This includes such opportunities as a sabbatical exchange between teachers and interns and use of the media center and curriculum library. "There is a growing recognition that there must be a redefinition of the responsibilities of the schools and the universities, the development of even closer relationships between the two, and allocation of costs so as not to place an undue hardship on either."*

*Report of the Professional Committee of the Five College Project, (mimeographed), Hamilton, New York 1968.

It implies involvement of administrators and others in on-going programs at the University through Study Councils and through research and evaluation Field Services Projects.

Professional Associations. The passing of the Taylor Law in 1968 and the State policy of giving more responsibility to teachers' associations for the development of their profession has provided incentive for greater cooperation between schools and Universities. The trend is for professional associations to assist the Universities in planning their teacher preparation programs, and for University representatives to serve, in turn, to help evaluate school programs. Professional associations may be constructive forces for bringing about change. They need no longer limit their concern to economic affairs.

Comments and Conclusion

Three "bottlenecks" might be mentioned:

1. Local school districts are short of funds, as reported by board members, parents, and others (see later chapters). There is strong competition among programs for existing funds. This makes it difficult to inaugurate a new program such as the Alliance. Innovations are often the first to be cut from the budget.

2. Universities, especially liberal arts ones, periodically question whether they should be involved in teacher preparation. During financial "crunches" they tend to reduce teacher preparation staff, even though little saving is involved. This impedes the continuity of a program such as the Alliance at a time when schools need to be reasonably assured that a supply of interns will be available and that other mutual arrangements will not suddenly fold.

3. State governments, when short on funds, may shift priorities, so that both schools and Universities could find their cooperative programs without support. Support through BOCES and the State Education Department, however, tends to be more stable than short-time grants from whatever source.

It seems, to those most closely involved, that the Alliance is a logical organizational structure through which mutual goals can be achieved. The time schedule for such an undertaking is long-range.

CHAPTER 4
THE INFLUENCE OF THE PROJECT ON THE UNIVERSITY

One cannot fully understand the influences of the Kettering Project without considering its impact on the University, not only on its facilities and procedures for the preparation of teachers, but especially on the relationships of the University to the schools. The latter includes changes in the concept of articulation (coordination) of programs and facilities between the schools and the University, and ideas for interchange of staff and students. We will first discuss changes that have taken place in the preparation of teachers with respect to:

a. facilities such as the media center, curriculum center, research library and closed circuit TV and micro-teaching facilities; and

b. joint utilization of school and University staff.

Second, we will discuss implications of a new articulation concept, including

a. interchange of staff; and

b. interchange of students.

Some of the project influences on the University and schools have already materialized into results and some are long-range or even speculative.

Changes In Teacher Preparation

Facilities. The experience of working with the schools and the new techniques has suggested new ways of preparing teachers. It became evident that appropriate physical resources and facilities were needed if prospective and innovating teachers were to be prepared for their new roles.

Curriculum Research Center. The University had previously developed one curriculum library and facility for English and social studies and a second for mathematics and science. In these were located numerous materials, such as syllabi, textbooks, and simulations, games and sample projects. They contained space for the participant to work and confer. These curriculum and medium materials were expanded as a result of the project.

Self-Instructional Media Center. Prior to the project, the University had no modern system of instructing inexperienced and experienced teachers in the new techniques and no adequate ways for them to prepare teaching materials. A 14' x 20' room was renovated and equipped as a self-instructional media center. It was equipped with five carrells with electrical outlets. These were used in conjunction with equipment so that up to five participants could work at the same time. A typewriter with special large type for making transparencies, a paper cutter, dry mounting press and other materials for production were also available. Colgate's self-instructional sequence was designed so that participants could progress in a step-by-step manner in learning to use the equipment and materials. Some of the equipment includes video tape recorder, audio tape recorders, 8 mm loop projector, filmstrip projector, 16 mm projector, overhead projector, record player, cassettes, a thermofax for preparation of transparencies, slides, audio tapes and dry mount apparatus. The self-instructional concept is not a new one to education. S.N. Posthlethwait has been using his "audio-tutorial" system in biology successfully for years at Purdue University. The self-instructional mode is used at many colleges for teaching the media material, as well as for learning the operation of equipment. Also, McGraw-Hill publishes a kit for this purpose, as will be discussed later.

Instruction begins with a video tape recorder which is arranged so that when the learner follows written directions he can activate the video screen. A diagram on the wall shows him how to thread the tape and play it back. The sequence that follows shows how to use or prepare materials with key pieces of equipment. For example, the first part demonstrates the use of the Kodak Carrousel Projector. While the tape is being played (or if the participant desires, he may replay the part), he actually operates the projector. Because he operates the equipment as he learns, he gains confidence in actual usage. He makes his errors free from criticism. At the end of part one, he has learned to operate the video tape recorder and the carrousel projector.

In all, six media are covered in the initial 20-minute video tape:
1. Carrousel projector,
2. 8 mm loop projector,
3. record player,
4. filmstrip projector,
5. filmstrip pre-viewer, and
6. the cassette tape recorder.

When the student has learned to use the carrousel, he may select one of three loaded cartridges which contain slides showing the use of the 16 mm projector, the Wolensack tape recorder, or the 8 mm film loop projector. Or, if he has learned the 8 mm projector, he may go to one of two collections of six cartridges each to demonstrate to himself how to make and use transparencies, use motion pictures, splice film or tape, or learn one of several other skills in which he is interested. (Prepared by Chandler Publishing Company and McGraw-Hill, respectively.) Or he may go to another loaded carrousel tray, carefully labeled, and use the McGraw-Hill Educational Media Kit (EMK). If he does this, he shows himself a series of approximately 30 slides, and finds himself referred to a separate kit on the one or more media he wishes to use. Each EMK kit has an audio tape, 8 mm and 16 mm loop, film, which the learner can load to demonstrate an example of media in which the participant is interested. The content is designed to teach the skill and the role of the particular technology in changing and improving education.

By using the original video tape, the participant learns at his own pace, reviewing as he goes along. He is able to skip over sequences in which he is competent and concentrate on weak areas. Since motor skills play an important role in equipment operation and preparation of materials, motion sequences from films and video tapes are used to teach them.

Educational Research Library. This library is a modern new conference room which is equipped with selected basic references, such as the *Encyclopedia of Educational Research,* Gage's *Handbook on Research in Teaching,* and the monthly ERIC Research in Education Abstracts. In the room is a micro-fiche (3M) reader on which the complete publications referred to in the ERIC abstract can be read or scanned. Selected pages can be automatically printed on 8½ x 11 copy paper. A complete file of ERIC micro-fiches is available from Che-Mad-Her-On for use in the machine. Because the library is such a new addition, use has not been fully determined. At present, it is open to all who request it.

The Closed Circuit TV Studio and Microteaching. The major uses of the closed circuit TV facilities are for microteaching, teaching of speech, and recording and playback of instructional material. Microteaching is the major use. All interns undergo an intensive period of small group teaching using video tape the summer prior to their actual teaching. Groups of six to eight pupils are taught 5 to 15 minute lessons designed to demonstrate one of fifteen to twenty techniques, such as non-verbal instruction and the use of thought questions. Intern supervisors discuss the results with the intern while viewing the video tape, and interns can view the videotape on their own in the media center. Several of the schools in the Kettering-Colgate Project used similar video tape equipment to improve instruction of experienced teachers. Several more asked the staff to demonstrate microteaching to groups of their faculty.

Previous to 1968 the University Department of Education had developed a TV studio using a 1" video tape recorder. It has since switched to ½" equipment which it has found to be more portable and dependable. The room is connected by cable to two other rooms, one large and one small, which, because of the connection, can also be used as studios. Equipment includes three complete ½" closed circuit systems for studio and classroom use, and three portable systems for recording outside of the studio complex. It is operated and maintained by a student supervisor and his team of five student assistants.

Articulation between Schools and University

Joint Utilization of School and University Professional Staffs. Two experimental programs in which University and school staff share time and talent to bring about change in both have been tried in 1970-71. The first was the Alliance of Schools plan described in Chapter 3. How does this change affect the University and school programs for teacher preparation?

For the University, it changes

1. the nature of the internship (and practice teacher) arrangement;
2. the methods courses; and
3. the manner of providing in-service training.

It also tends to equalize the status relationship between the University and school faculty. When the Sherburne-Earlville Central School District joined the Alliance, it agreed to employ two graduate interns each semester where only one teacher's position existed previously plus two other interns. This reduced the teaching load of both the interns and the departmental faculty members, providing the additional time needed for curriculum planning, and for the interns to learn. This made the expanded staff only a little more expensive than the old system.

The interns did not teach in a self-contained classroom as they normally would have done; rather they taught as members of the departmental team at the grade levels in which the curriculum was to be changed. They taught (large groups or small groups) or worked on plans, depending on their talents and the needs of the whole department. The school arranged the pupil schedule so that at certain times all the departmental staff could meet. Further, a paid week for planning was scheduled before school started. Arrangements were more conducive to the development of teacher leadership qualities and for learning to implement new curricula and methods, both for the interns and for the experienced teachers.

The second program was an arrangement for Colgate Seniors with one of the teachers of the Hamilton Central School, in which the latter participated with the University professor in teaching the social studies methods class, and the students served as team members with him in the teaching program.

Both of these programs differed from the existing program in that faculty members of school and University worked together with prospective teachers at the University and at the school. Both have implications for new roles for the experienced teachers and the University faculty members. For example, it would be possible for selected teachers to have an arrangement with the University so that they would be responsible for supervising the interns. At the same time, the present

University supervisor and professor roles might be merged. This might free time for more consultant work and planning, not only between school and University, but among the schools. Also, the suggestion has been made that the Alliance schools consider making definite arrangements for the exchange of staff among schools for short periods, so that teachers could benefit by actually experiencing working in other new programs. Such an exchange might accelerate the diffusion of innovations in the give-and-take of the process.

Two other aspects tended to change:

1. the roles of the professors and the University supervisors; and
2. the nature of the in-service "courses" for experienced teachers.

Normally, the University professor would teach his methods class and help supervise the graduate intern. Most of the visitation, however, would have been done by the intern supervisor. Under the Alliance plan, the professor and the supervisor were on a clinical team with the teachers of the appropriate school department. Second, where formerly the experienced teacher registered for short workshops or enrolled for inservice courses to upgrade his competencies, he now was engaged in a continuous inservice program during the entire academic year. He had status as an equal. A third aspect could be brought in, but has not been used as yet. High school students could become involved in helping the faculty understand the teaching-learning process, and thus to understand it themselves.

Interchange of Students. Not only can the role of school and University faculty members be interchanged; students can and do interchange. High achieving students in high school enroll for University study during the summers, or late afternoons. Indeed, over 500 do this now each year at Colgate University, except that they do not receive credit. They do it voluntarily.

Formalized exchange programs for university students are increasing in number. Each semester as many as 40 Colgate University students exchange with students from six selected colleges.

The concept of exchange of students can be extended to include the disadvantaged college-bound. Colgate University and five other colleges have developed a Higher Education Opportunity Program (HEOP) in which 60 to 100 disadvantaged college-bound high school seniors enroll for two courses of college credit, during six weeks of Summer Session, preceding entrance to college. This experience tends to increase their readiness for college study and makes possible a reduced load during the Freshman year. The program extends the student exchange idea beyond the one previously described. Participating students may apply for admission to any of the six colleges (or any other college). After admission, they may exchange a semester or may transfer between colleges or from one of the five to a two-year college, or vice versa without loss of credit or student aid. Financial aspects are arranged under the supervision of a Consortium Board of Directors of representatives from the colleges. *Currents,* a recent ERIC bulletin (Number 3, November, 1970) discusses this whole trend toward interchange of students.

Thought has even been given to a plan in which the division between secondary school and university levels would be replaced by a plan in which able high school students would accelerate. This would lead to a removal of the division between levels, secondary and university, for them. It might be an advantage to all concerned to have secondary students and university students studying on the same campus, teaching and learning from each other. University students these days are very much interested in teaching and advising younger students.

Conversely, college students could devote a semester to off-campus study in selected schools. This plan is the reverse of the former; it encourages college students to live in the local school district, rather than high school students to come to the campus. This is not absurd. Colgate University now has one black undergraduate student studying two related courses and teaching for one semester off-campus, in a ghetto area, under such a plan. As discussed in the November 1970 ERIC *Currents,* more and more college students are participating in off-campus study, or taking a complete break for a semester or a year, to do something else. *Currents* quotes Dorothy Knoell as saying, "A college attendance pattern is recommended which would include systematic breaks and return points, either between high school and college or during college." At Colgate University, for as many as 200 students, four years is not the normal progression to graduation. When one considers the preceding changes in the former lock-step system of education, the phrase "articulation between school and college" can take on new meanings.

CHAPTER 5
RESTRUCTURING vs. THE "RIPPLE" APPROACH

At the close of Phase III of the project (June 5, 1970), innovating teachers completed an inventory called "An Evaluation of the Innovative Experience." (See Exhibit V-1.) The inventory served three major purposes:

1. to record the innovating teachers' judgment on the issue of whether a redesign approach would have been more effective than the gradual approach used in this project,
2. to assess the extent of diffusion, and
3. to determine the perceived effectiveness of that experience.

Other data were then employed to determine the awareness of the ripple by other faculty members.

Re-Design vs. The Gradual "Ripple" Approach

Innovating Teacher Reaction. The innovators were presented with the following issue: some educational theorists believe that restructuring the school is more important for encouraging innovation than any "ripple" effect that one innovation can produce. When asked to give their reaction to this belief, on the basis of their knowledge and experience, half (14 out of 27) responded in favor of the "ripple", and gave their reasons, such as:

1. "It's the staff and personnel that makes or breaks the innovation."
2. "The staff must feel the need to have the desire for change." "The 'ripple' begins on firmer ground."
3. "I don't believe that it is feasible in most cases to completely restructure the school. Change must be a slow evolutionary process."
4. "I don't believe we can move toward innovation 'en masse' and still make it an effective learning opportunity."
5. "I know for a fact that several teachers were influenced by our endeavors to do something to keep up with our department."

Those agreeing (favoring restructuring):

1. "Modular scheduling would add tremendously to the possibilities for further innovation."
2. "'Ripples' are targets for criticism and resentment."
3. "The interest of all areas must be developed before individuals will dare a change."
4. "A great majority of teachers would be involved to produce many 'ripples'."
5. "The ripples are not enough to move people who have been in a rut. A stronger force is needed."

The innovating teachers were then asked, "which approach would you recommend to change agents in other schools?" Seventy percent (19 out of 27) favored a combination; 22 percent favored the "ripple" approach; and 8 percent favored the restructuring approach. Reasons for combining were: "It would reduce the risk due to an extreme change." "Combination provides for initiative and individuality on the part of the innovator." " 'Ripples' need reinforcing." "The approach would depend on the nature of the school and its constituents." " Even with restructuring, individual innovators would be needed."

The teachers were then asked "What do you see as the positive and negative aspects of the 'ripple' effect (the techniques used in the Kettering Project)?"

Positive:

"Any changes worth making and proved to be effective and flexible will spread."

"It is contagious."

"Change by 'infection' is more successful than change by edict."

Negative:

"Without outside encouragement, it is difficult to manage scheduling, room space and equipment to put new ideas and projects into motion."

"Too 'piece-meal' an effort sometimes will fail because it is placed in the same old structural system."

"Some teachers are immune."

What these innovating teachers seem to be telling us is that there is a need to change outmoded, lock-step systems of education. However, they perceive a great deal of resistance by school personnel, board members, parents and others. When the "ripple" effect is used alone, its ripples may become overwhelmed by habitual patterns. Continual diffusion and reinforcement efforts for the innovative project are needed. If left to itself, the innovation will have difficulty with scheduling and physical arrangements and may even lead to resentment by other teachers. Administrative and faculty support are needed. (The Kettering Project provided this reinforcement for three years.) The "ripple" approach may not have a weakness as designed. However, breakdowns in design may bring about weaknesses such as those mentioned above: lack of dissemination, lack of school administration and faculty support. Those who prefer a combination, say that they want more rapid change than provided by the "ripple" approach.

Diffusion of Ideas by the Innovating Teacher

As indicated in the preceding section, diffusion seems to be one important element for the success of the "ripple" effect. Table V-1 shows the frequency of diffusion by the innovating teacher. The 27 teachers met 316 times with individuals to explain their innovations, for an average of 11 each, and with groups, they met 157 times, for an average of 5 times each. They discussed the innovation most frequently with students and colleagues. Five of the innovating teachers arranged an average of two group meetings each with school board members. Nineteen arranged no group school board meetings. (The diffusion activity was voluntary.)

Hypothesis. The extent of diffusion of innovations through individual and group meetings by the innovating teacher is significantly related to the criteria.

TABLE V-1 The Relation of Diffusion by the Innovating Teacher
to the Criteria. (N = 27)

Diffusion	Means	Effect on Schools (Pearson's r) Attitude (Post-)	Availability (Post-)	Usage (Post-)
Number of meetings with individuals	10.9	.41	--	--
Number of meetings with groups	5.4		.53	.32

TABLE V-2 Verbal Description of the Meaning of the
Correlation Coefficient* (Pearson's r)

Size of the Coefficient	Verbal Description
Less than .2	Slight, almost negligible relationship
.2 to .4	Low r, definite but small relationship
.4 to .7	Moderate r, substantial relationship
.7 to .9	High r, marked relationship
.9 to 1.0	Very high r, very dependable relationship

These descriptions apply when the size of the sample is in the vicinity of 70 or greater. If N is in the vicinity of 26, correlation of .38 is needed before one could say that there was a definite (but small) relationship.

*Guilford, p. 145

Discussion of Evidence. To check the claim that diffusion is a force in making for effective change, a diffusion score was calculated for each innovator. This score was the total number of times he met with individuals and groups to explain his innovation. (Preliminary analysis indicated that a total frequency was more predictive than the number of individual or group meetings alone.) The diffusion score for each school was then correlated with its usage, availability and attitude indexes. (The criteria for this study.) Table V-1 shows that the amount of diffusion was significantly related to two of the criteria; the faculty's post-attitude (r = .41) and the availability of innovations in the school (r = .53). (See Table V-2.) It was not related to gains. Dissemination to individuals seemed to be related to attitude, and dissemination to groups to availability.

Therefore, the question should be raised as to whether the diffusion of innovations dissemination influenced the schools to change, or whether it was easier for the innovator to disseminate in a school in which the faculty had a more favorable attitude and in which more innovative opportunities were available. In any event, the variable - amount of dissemination by the innovating teacher - is one of the forces that will be selected in a later study summarizing the relative importance of several influencing variables.

The Effectiveness of Training Program

The innovating teachers gave much time to preparation. They devoted thirty-two hours to "becoming comfortable with the innovation" during the first semester, in addition to the summer workshop time. They rated both the summer training period and the first semester on-the-job consultant services as being quite useful. Their attitude toward the innovations remained positive throughout the three years of the study. None shifted to a negative attitude. Seventeen of the twenty-seven rated their innovation "quite" or "very" effective in developing student motivation, as contrasted to the usual motivational techniques. None said "Not at all" effective.

Awareness of the Ripple Effect by Other Teachers in the School

Another important element necessary before the ripple approach could be effective is that other teachers in the school be aware that an experiment is in progress, and recognize it as a new approach. To ascertain the reality that a ripple effect was in operation, a single, experimental design was created. All school personnel were asked, at the end of phase III, the question: "Which department in the school do you believe has been the most innovative during the past two years?"

They named the department in an open-ended question. This response was then compared to the department in which the Kettering project was located to see whether there was significant agreement. Table V-3 shows the results. It should be read as follows: "One hundred forty-seven teachers named the English Department as the most innovative; of these, eighty-two were in schools where the Kettering Project was in the English Department; twenty-one were in schools where the project was in the Mathematics Department; sixteen were in the Science Department and twelve in the Social Studies Department.

Hypothesis. The Department in which the Kettering Project was located was considered by the professional school personnel to be the most innovative department in the school.

Discussion of Evidence. Table V-3 shows that without exception the greatest number of faculty members agreed that the Kettering-Colgate Project was in the most innovative department. The Chi square of 262.6 is much greater than would be obtained by chance. When converted to a coefficient of contingency, the relationship becomes more evident (C = .57). See Conclusion 4 for further discussion.

TABLE V-3 The Extent to which the Kettering Project Innovation was in the Department Considered to be the Most Innovative in the School (As reported by all the teachers).

Department in which the Kettering Project was Located	Teachers' Response as to which Department was Most Innovative (Frequencies)				
	English	Math.	Science	Social Studies	Other
English	82	5	8	28	19
Mathematics	21	21	5	11	11
Science	16	12	66	32	26
Social Studies	12	4	2	44	15
General School Innovation (e.g. Improvement of Instruction through Closed Circuit TV analysis)	16	18	50	21	13
TOTALS	147	66	131	136	84

Chi Square = 262.6   Needed Chi Square at .05 level (26.3) N = 564

Conclusions.
1. Innovating teachers, after two years of participation in the project, tend to support a combination of the "ripple" and restructuring approach to bring about educational change. In their judgment, the ripple approach is effective in that the initiative and responsibility is placed where it belongs—with the person who is to do the innovating. Imposed innovations may destroy the creativity of the teacher. Restructuring, if combined with the "ripple" approach, gives the innovative teacher needed moral support, encouragement and facilities.
2. Diffusion of the innovation by the innovating teacher is significantly related to two of the criteria: the number of meetings with individuals is definitely

27

related to faculty attitude, and the frequency of group meetings to availability. This may mean that diffusion was easier to promote in schools with a more favorable faculty attitude and more innovations available.

3. Innovating teachers rated the operation of the program as "quite" or "very" effective. They devoted much time and effort to assisting in its success.

4. At the end of the experimental period, the department in which the Kettering Project innovation was located tended to be considered the most innovative department in the school. This was especially true for the English, science and social studies projects, and less true for the mathematics projects. A Chi-Square of 262.6 was obtained, compared to one of 26.3 or greater needed to substantiate the hypothesis at the .05 level of probability. (See Table V-3.)

This finding tends to substantiate the existence of a "ripple effect". If teachers identified, as the most innovative, some department different than the one in which the innovating teacher was located, the study would have concluded that the "ripples" were indeed weak or non-existent. The evidence does not necessarily mean that the intervention of the project caused the department to be considered the most innovative. There are other influences operating. It does mean that the faculty tended to perceive the most innovative department to be the one in which the intervention project (the experimental variable) was located.

Exhibit V-1 An Evaluation of the Innovational Experience

Your name_____

1. Diffusion

1. How many times have you met with the following, _____
   for the purpose of explaining your innovations? (Check the appropriate category for each entry)

   Number of Occasions

	4 or more	3	2	1	0
as individuals					
staff members of your school					
staff members at other schools					
students in your school*					
parents					
school board members					
as groups					
staff members of your school					
students in your school*					
parents					
school board members					

2. Has the example provided by your innovation influenced others to innovate?

         yes   no   undecided

   Please explain

II. Preparation

3. How useful to you was the training provided by the project? (Circle one letter)
   A) Very B) Quite C) A moderate amount D) Somewhat E) Not at all

28

4. How useful were the consulting services provided by the Project?
   A) Very B) Quite C) A moderate amount D) Somewhat E) Not at all
5. How many hours of personal effort did it take you during the first semester of its use to become comfortable with your innovation?
   A) Less than 10 B) 10-20 C) 21-30 D) 31-40 E) 40 or more

III. Opinions

6. In your opinion how effective was your innovation in developing student motivation in contrast to your usual motivational techniques?
   A) Not at all B) Somewhat C) Moderately D) Quite E) Very
7. Has your attitude toward the innovation changed?   Yes   No
   If "Yes", how much and in which direction?
   A) Very positive B) Quite Positive C) About equally positive and negative
        D) Quite Negative E) Very Negative
8. Some educational theorists believe that restructuring the school is more important for encouraging innovation than any "ripple" effect that one innovation can produce.

   On the basis of your knowledge and experience, what is your reaction to this belief?   Agree   Disagree
   Please explain your choice:

   Which approach would you recommend to change agents in other schools?
           Restructuring   ripple**   a combination
   Why?

   What do you see as the positive and negative aspects of the "ripple" effect (the technique encouraged by this Project)?
   Positive

   Negative

*Other than those directly involved.   **ripple = gradual spread

29

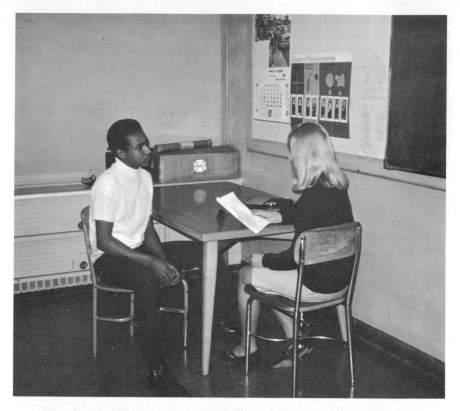

Student participation in innovative projects tended to reduce friction.

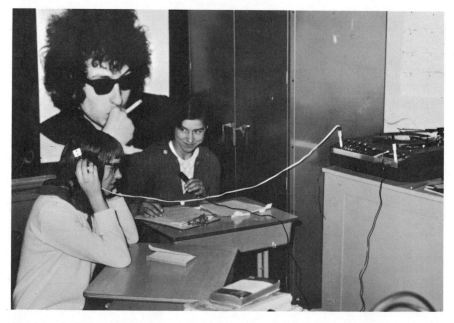

Students in innovative schools were more aware of their goals — humanities project.

PART II
RESEARCH

Resource teachers plan together for the effective introduction of innovations.

Introduction

The most important step in any research study that intends to identify the elements or forces related to success, is the definition of the criteria for that success in measurable terms. This is true whether one is trying to predict grades, attitudes, skill, economic gain or educational change. The need for an accurate way of knowing whether the intervention of the experimental elements or forces have been successful is crucial. For example, we need to know whether community forces such as the attitude of parents and board members had any influence on educational change in the schools. We need to know whether financial resources of the district were an impeding factor as suspected, and whether administrative leadership in introducing innovation was a significant force. Without a reliable and valid criteria, research would be limited to a descriptive study simply listing normative elements as: whether parents and board members were favorable or unfavorable toward innovations, whether they voted at school meetings frequently or did not. We could not have determined whether these elements were important influences on educational change.

For this reason, considerable attention is given in this report to the process of defining of the criteria, constructing the measures of the criteria and studying their validity and reliability.

The major, overall research objective of the project was to study community and school forces impeding and facilitating change in attitudes, availability and usage of innovations (the criteria) in twenty-six schools. This objective was to be attained by effectively introducing innovations in each of the experimental schools and then measuring the influences of the forces (variables) on the criteria-attitudes, availability and usage. Actually, this procedure made it possible to use two types of experimental designs to be described later.

Definition and Measurement of the Criteria Variables

Six criteria* were employed to measure innovation and changes in innovation in the twenty-six schools.

1. Faculty Attitude toward Innovation: the extent to which all of the school personnel, faculty members and administration were favorable or unfavorable toward a group of defined innovations, as measured by a ten-item Thurstone-Likert attitudes scale.
   Sample Items (Favorable and Unfavorable):
   − An attempt to innovate represents one of the most dynamic advances a school system can make.
   − These innovations do not impress me favorably.
2. Change in Faculty Attitude Toward Innovations: the difference in each school's favorableness toward innovations (on criterion 1) in 1968 and the faculty attitude two years later in 1970.
3. Availability of Innovations in Each School: the extent to which curricular, technological, structural and other innovations, such as team teaching, and

---

*Hereafter, in this report, to simplify the discussion, the criteria will be referred to as (1) Attitude; (2) Gain in Attitude; (3) Availability; (4) Gain in Availability; (5) Usage, (6) Gain in Usage.

learning centers, were available (as measured by a team of two raters using the Hamilton Innovation Profile Instrument (HIP).

Sample Item: Does the school provide wet carrells for independent study?

4. Change in Availability of Innovations: the difference in each school on the HIP Instrument from Pre-survey time two years later (1970).

5. Usage of Innovations in Each School: the level of sophistication of usage of curricular and technological, structural and other innovations, such as team teaching and learning centers, as measured by the team of two raters, using the HIP instrument at the same time they were rating the school for criteria 3.

Sample Item: Did students use wet carrells for independent study?

6. Change in Usage of Innovations in Each School: the difference (gain or loss) each school made on the HIP instrument over the same two-year period (1968 to 1970).

These definitions are provided as aids in simplifying later discussion of the effect of the forces on school innovation (the criterion). Included above is a brief mention of how each of the criteria was measured. For a fuller discussion of these criterion instruments, see Appendix B. Definitions of school and community forces (the independent variables) and information on the other measuring instruments will be presented there. Selection, preparation and analysis of appropriate instruments, are important parts of the study (see validity and reliability of instruments in Appendix B).

Variable 1 (Action or Attitude)

Variable 2

Variable 3 ⟶ Significant Observed Effects On One or More of the Six Criteria.

Variable 4

Etc.

Figure VI-1* The Correlation Design: Chains of Inter-relationship among Attitudes and Actions and their Influence on the Criteria (Design I)

Research Design I

Pre- and post-survey measures were obtained for each of the criteria and for each independent variable (school and community force**). Individual responses

---

*For example, Figure VI-1 might read as follows: Variable 1, such as knowledge about the Kettering-Colgate Project, influences faculty attitude toward modernization (Variable 2). This in turn influences the faculty to try more innovation (Variable 3). The fact that more new practices are being tried in one school then another is then observed as a fact by outside raters visiting the schools (the criterian variable, such as usage, see box on right side).

**Pre- and post-measures of the independent variables were not always needed. (For example, years of service on the Board of Education.) Also, in some cases only a post-measure was relevant (e.g., the influence of the Kettering Project).

were combined to form 26 school means for each variable. The means were indexes of the standing of each school on the criteria and on the independent variables (school-community forces). Correlation coefficients were then calculated to identify the extent of linkage of events (actions and attitudes) to the consequence standing of the school with respect to the criteria (innovation in the school). Correlation coefficients between the forces and the criteria are among schools. Those between forces are among individuals (parents, pupils, board members, teachers and administrators). Significant correlation coefficients among the independent variables identify chains or sequences of actions or attitudes (forces). Correlations between the independent variables and the criteria identify which chain of events have significant impact on innovation in the schools (see Figure VI-1 for graphic illustration). Forces which show significant relationships to the criteria will be used later in a multiple correlation and regression design (Design III) to study their relative importance for school innovation and the extent to which they account for the differences among the schools in this respect.

In addition to this basic design (Design I), other statistical methods such as factor analysis and non-parametric procedures will be used to analyze the research instruments and the nominal scale data respectively. Also, a separate study will be made using an interview case study approach (Design IV). A brief comparison of the effectiveness of the four designs will be made in Appendix D.

Rationale For Design I with Respect to the Impact of the Effective Introduction of the Innovations in the Experimental Schools. Two types of conclusions can be drawn from the first design. If the independent variables are related to change during the two-year period, they can be called school or community forces attributable to the intervention of the Kettering Project or of some other influence during the two years. If, however, they are related only to the post-survey criteria (attitude, availability and usage) they are school and community forces but not necessarily related to the experiment (intervention by this project). Probably, they are forces that have had impact over a longer period of time. For example, if parents in a community believe that they should pressure the administration for modernization and this is related to usage in the school (see Figure VII-1), but not to gain in usage during the two-year period, then such parental pressure did not cause the school to change during the experiment. It was, however, related to the level of usage that the school had attained. It still could be a community force. Thus, there are two purposes in identifying the forces: 1. to determine whether the "ripple approach" used by this project had a significant influence, and if so, what forces were at work during the use of the "ripple approach" that influenced change during the project; and 2. to determine what school and community forces had a long-range influence on the criteria or had been at work before 1968.

Research Design II

As previously discussed, Design II asks the question, "How much did the experimental group of schools gain on the criteria and was this gain greater than that of the control group (or comparison school)?" Unlike Design I, this design does not inquire with great depth into why some experimental schools gained more than others. In other words, it does not study the forces at work. It does, however, present important evidence.

Hypotheses Design II:

1. The twenty-six experimental schools would gain significantly more than the eleven control schools in faculty attitude toward Innovation (criteria 1 and 2). To test this hypothesis a ten-item scale (the ATI) was administered to all the faculty of the experimental and control schools in 1968, and in 1970.
2. The experimental and control groups would be significantly above the neutral point in favorableness toward innovations at the close of the experiment.
3. The experimental group would gain more in availability and usage than the comparison school group.

The purpose of Design II is to determine whether the experimental group (twenty-six schools) gained more on the criteria than did the eleven control schools. In other words, did the intervention of the experimental variable, the introduction of innovations into the experimental schools, produce overall gain on the criteria greater than gains made by the control schools. The design is illustrated in Figure VI-2.

Measures of only two of the six criteria were available for the ten-school control group, Attitude and Attitude change. Distance prohibited visitations for rating of the usage and availability criteria. As a substitute for the latter, raters visited one school not in the experiment, to provide a base line for both their pre- and post-rating visits. This school will be called "the comparison school." After familiarizing themselves with this school and agreeing as to its standing on the HIP, the two observers visited the twenty-six experimental schools and rated each of them using the "comparison school" as a base line. Two years later, at post-survey time, two raters again visited the "comparison school," rated it, and used its standing on the HIP with respect to availability and usage, as a base line for the post-rating of the twenty-six schools. Pre- and Post-criteria ratings for the "comparison school" were thus available for comparison with the ratings of the experimental schools. The final effect was similar to having a control group of one school for the other four criteria.

Results of the study, using Design I, are presented in Chapters 7 through 10. Design II results appear in Appendix A.

TIME SEQUENCE

	1968			**1970**
Experimental Group (26 Schools)	Pre-Survey ➤	Exposure to Experimental Variable	➤	Post-Survey
Control Group (10 Schools and one comparison school)	Pre-Survey ➤	– – – – – – ➤		Post-Survey

Figure VI-2 The Pre-Post Test Experimental Control Group Design (Design II) *

---

*For further information see: Donald T. Campbell and Julian C. Stanley, *Experimental and Quasi-Experimental Designs for Research,* Rand McNally & Company, Chicago, Ill. 1966.

33

Influence of Parents

Theory: The influence of the public on school boards and administrators has been discussed by a number of writers, including Brickell and Miles. Brickell states that the power of citizens is limited to influencing the "climate of interest," which may lead indirectly to innovation in the school. He says, "Parents' and citizens' groups in most communities do not exert a direct influence on the adoption of new types of instructional programs, probably because they do not know enough about educational methodology to favor or oppose specific innovations. Their influence is ordinarily limited to creating a climate of interest – or lack of it – in better results."*

If Brickell's theory is accurate, this research study would expect to find that school districts in which parents were (1) better informed and more favorable toward innovation would have a favorable climate of interest and as a consequence; (2) their schools would be relatively advanced in innovation (availability and usage). The present project included Brickell's two variables and several others in its study. What are its findings? Do they support, negate, or expand the theory with respect to the forces exerted by parents?

Community Forces (Definitions and Sample Items from BOPAR (Board-Parent Survey).

Parent Power
   A. Variables (Attitudes and Actions):
      1. Information on Innovation in the schools. (Self-report)
         a. How much do you know about innovation at the local secondary school?
            A. Very little
            B. Little
            C. Some
            D. Considerable
            E. A great deal
      2. Attitude Toward Modernization (Self-report)
         a. How important to your community is it that the local secondary school be up-to-date in its ways of educating students?
            A. Very little
            B. Little
            C. Some
            D. Considerable
            E. A great deal
      3. Voting at School Meetings (Frequency)
         a. How often do you exercise your right to vote at annual school elections?
            A. Never
            B. Sometimes
            C. Often
            D. Very often
            E. Always

*Henry M. Brickell, *Organizing New York State for Educational Change,* The University of the State of New York, State Education Department, Albany, 1961, p. 20.

4. Parental Pressure on School for Innovation.
   a. In your opinion, how much pressure should parents in your community exert to have innovations introduced into the local secondary school?
      A. Very little
      B. Little
      C. Some
      D. Considerable
      E. A great deal
5. Pressure on Administration for Innovation.
   a. How important to you is it that the administrators of the secondary school be persons who actively work to support change and innovation?
      A. Not at all
      B. Somewhat
      C. Moderately
      D. Quite
      E. Very

B. Variable (Community)
   1. Financial Resources of District (Parental perception).
      a. In your opinion, how adequate are local financial resources for supporting innovations?
         A. Very inadequate
         B. Quite inadequate
         C. About equally adequate and inadequate
         D. Quite adequate
         E. Very adequate

Hypotheses. This study hypothesizes that these variables, including both parental attitude toward modernization and parental action are associated with innovation. It implies in these hypotheses that the variables might combine into a chain of events to bring about innovation.

The three major hypotheses for parents were:

1. Parental information about school innovations, attitude toward school modernization, voting at school meetings, and favorable attitudes toward exerting pressure in the community and for an innovative administration, will tend to form a sequence or chain of attitudes and actions that make a difference in the school.
2. Parental attitude toward modernization will be found to be the center of the chain of attitudes and actions and as such is significantly related to availability and usage of innovations in the school.
3. Parental perception of the financial resources of the district will be related to the criteria.

The Evidence and Discussion. Table VII-1 provides supporting evidence for the second hypothesis. Parental Attitude toward modernization is related to Availability and Usage (r's = .49 and .52, columns 1 and 2). Further study of Table VII-1 suggests that constructive, indirect influence on the local school results from parents who are more liberally inclined (parents who view teachers' salary negotiations as a positive force in shaping the community attitudes and who are better satisfied with the kind of education their children are receiving).

Figure VII-1 supports the first hypothesis; namely, that there are significant interrelationships or sequence chains among attitudes and actions. For example, favorableness of parental attitude toward modernization is related to information (r = .35), and is, in turn, associated with voting and other actions. The attitude toward modernization is the central force that is associated with the criteria-availability and usage. This means that parents with a more favorable attitude toward modernization become better informed, take more action, and that the resulting community climate produced by the parental attitudes has an indirect influence.

In addition, Table VII-1 supports the third hypothesis — Financial resources of the district — as perceived by the parents, is significantly related to availability (r = .50). Financial ability is not, however, a part of the chain of events and not related to the parent's attitude toward modernization or innovation.

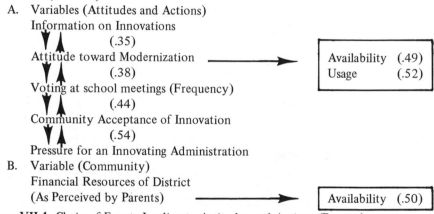

Effect on Innovations
in School Program
(Pearson's r)
(N = 26)

By Parents: (N = 876)
    A.   Variables (Attitudes and Actions)
        Information on Innovations
              (.35)
        Attitude toward Modernization   Availability (.49)
              (.38)   Usage   (.52)
        Voting at school meetings (Frequency)
              (.44)
        Community Acceptance of Innovation
              (.54)
        Pressure for an Innovating Administration
    B.   Variable (Community)
        Financial Resources of District
        (As Perceived by Parents)   Availability (.50)

Figure VII-1. Chain of Events Leading to Attitudes and Actions (Parents)

Conclusions and Implications.

1.   Information on new ideas and techniques used in the local school, may lead parents to form favorable attitudes toward innovations and modernization (or vice versa). This attitude tends to be associated with voting at school meetings (r = .38); and tends to lead to parental pressure in the community for school innovations (r = .44 and .45); and (probably indirectly) to pressure for innovative administration (r = .54). The attitude toward modernization is, in turn, related to the availability and usage of innovations in the school (r = .49 and .53, respectively.)

2.   The financial resources of the district for supporting innovations (parental perception) is an important force making for differences in availability of innovations among the schools (r = .50).

Table VII-1. Relation of Community Forces (Parents) to Relative Standing of Schools on Two Innovation Criteria

	PARENTS	
	(r survey items vs. criteria)	
	Avail. (Post)	Usage (Post)
1. Attitude toward Modernization	.49	.52
2. Community Desire for Quality Education (Pre & Post)	.41 & .39	.52 & .30
3. Perception of Community Acceptance of New (Pre & Post)	.46*	—
4. Financial Resources of District	.50	—
5. Attitude Toward Teachers' Negotiations	.31	—
6. Satisfaction with School (Post)	—	.45
7. Parental Pressure for an Innovative Administration	—	.47

*An r of .38 or better is needed for significance at the .05 level.

Schools will be more successful in modernization if the parents have a favorable attitude toward them. Associated with this favorable parental attitude are: (1) being well-informed about new ideas and techniques used in the school, (2) frequency of voting at school meetings, and (3) pressure for an innovative administration. In schools with a favorable parental group, modern practices will tend to be available and used more. Results of this study indicate that parents have more indirect influence on change than has been attributed to them. They learn about new practices from their children, talk about them to others and provide feedback to the administration and faculty, and vote at school meetings.

A separate force that may impede modernization, is parental perception of financial resources. One way to impede change is for the administration and board members to emphasize to parents the existence of a financial "crunch".

Board Members

Influence of Board Members. Brickell states that "the Board of Education in most communities is not a strong agent in determining the pattern of educational innovation, but its influence is decisive when exerted."* He says that the role of the Board of Education is much like that of the general public in that they are important sources of demand for improved outcomes, but rarely demands for specific instructional innovations.

If the theory is accurate, this research study should find that board member influence is similar to parent influence. Schools having boards with a favorable attitude toward modernization should be more advanced in innovation. Brickell might also have pointed to the board's concept of its role; namely its responsiveness to parental and community pressures. This study included these and other variables, as follows.

Community Forces (Definitions and Sample Items from BOPAR):

Board Members' Power:

A. Variables (Attitudes and Actions):

*Henry Brickell, *Organizing New York State for Educational Change,* University of the State of New York, State Education Department, Albany, 1961, p. 21

1. Community Desire for Modernizations:
    a. How important to your community is it that the local secondary school try new ways of educating students?
        A. Not at all
        B. Somewhat
        C. Moderately
        D. Quite
        E. Very
2. Community Acceptance of Innovations:
    a. Which phrase best describes your community's rate of acceptance of innovations at the secondary school level?
        A. Very slow
        B. Rather slow
        C. About equally slow and rapid
        D. Rather rapid
        E. Very rapid
3. Extent to which the School is Responsive to the Community Attitude:
    a. In your opinion, how responsive is the local secondary school to the community's attitude toward innovation?
        A. Not at all
        B. Somewhat
        C. Moderately
        D. Quite
        E. Very

B. Variables (Characteristics: (Board and Community) (Financial Resources of District)
    1. Financial Resources of District:
        a. (Same as variable B-2 for Parents)
    2. Maturity of Board (Age and Years of Service):
        a. How many years have you served on the school board?
            A. Less than 2
            B. 2 – 5
            C. 6 – 9
            D. 10 – 12
            E. More than 12
        b. What is your age in years, approximately?
            A. Under 21
            B. 21 – 35
            C. 36 – 50
            D. 51 – 65
            E. Over 65
    3. Socio-Economic Status of Board Members:
        a. What is the highest level you have reached in school?
            A. Less than a high school diploma
            B. A high school diploma
            C. More than a high school but less than a college diploma
            D. A college diploma
            E. More than a college diploma

b. How would you describe your financial situation in relation to the approximate national family average ($6,000 − $8,000)?
   A. Much less than average
   B. Less than average
   C. Average
   D. More than average
   E. Much more than average

4. Attitude toward modernization:
   a. How important to your community is it that the local secondary school be up-to-date in its ways of educating students?
      A. Very little
      B. Little
      C. Some
      D. Considerable
      E. A great deal

This study hypothesized that board member attitudes influence school innovations and in addition they perceive themselves as having an additional role, being responsive to the community attitudes. It is possible that this responsiveness results in the community attitude dominating over their own attitudes. The school board may thus reflect the community's attitude and not that of individual board members.

Hypotheses. Five major and two ancillary hypotheses relating to board members were tested:

1. Board members' attitude toward modernization is significantly related to the criteria.
2. Their attitude toward modernization may be the center of a chain of perceptions
3. Board members' perception of community acceptance of innovations is significantly related to the criteria.
4. Board members' perception of· community acceptance of innovations is the center of the sequence of perceptions and as such is the only one significantly related to the criteria.
5. Adequacy of financial resources for innovation (as perceived) is significantly related to the criteria.

Ancillary Hypotheses were:

6. Maturity of board members (years of service) is significantly related to the criteria.
7. Socio-economic status of board members is significantly related to the criteria.

Evidence and Discussion. Table VII-2 provided evidence for the first hypothesis. Correlations between attitude toward modernization and the criteria are .22 or less. Therefore the first and second experimental hypotheses must be rejected. Attitude toward modernization is not the central force in school board influence. What then is?

Table VII-2 also shows that board members' perception of the extent to which the community accepts innovations is significantly related to two of the criteria. If the board perceives the community to be favorable, the school tends to stand higher in availability and usage of innovations. The third hypothesis must be accepted.

Figure VII-2 supports the fourth hypothesis — that the board members' perception of the community's acceptance of innovations is related to his attitude toward modernization (r = .36) and to his view of whether the school is responsive to the community attitude (r = .44).

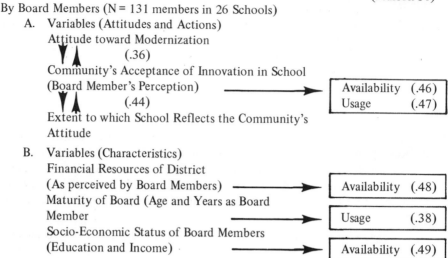

Effect on Innovation
In School Programs
(Pearson's r)

By Board Members (N = 131 members in 26 Schools)
  A. Variables (Attitudes and Actions)
      Attitude toward Modernization
                      (.36)
      Community's Acceptance of Innovation in School
      (Board Member's Perception)   → | Availability   (.46) |
                      (.44) | Usage   (.47) |
      Extent to which School Reflects the Community's
      Attitude

  B. Variables (Characteristics)
      Financial Resources of District
      (As perceived by Board Members)   → | Availability   (.48) |
      Maturity of Board (Age and Years as Board
      Member   → | Usage   (.38) |
      Socio-Economic Status of Board Members
      (Education and Income)   → | Availability   (.49) |

Figure VII-2. Chain of Events Leading to Attitudes and Actions (Board Members)

These conclusions expand somewhat on Brickell's statement. It would appear that the Board of Education influence on a school system's innovativeness is significant (r = .46 and .47). This influence does not seem to depend so much on members' own attitude (r = .09 and .22) as on their perception of the communities' attitude. They view their role as making the school responsive to the community (r = .44). This finding has implications for those who desire educational change. Influencing parental and community attitudes toward modernization may be one of the keys. Rather than "disseminating new programs in a manner which will not arouse the opposition of Boards of Education," they should be disseminated in a way that will arouse parental support.

There is evidence from a different source that school board members are "in tune" with the attitudes of parents. When school district means were compared, a close relationship was found (r - .38) between the "attitude toward innovation" of school board members and parents. If a district's parents are favorable, the board members tend to be favorable. There was no similar relationship with the attitudes of school professionals. The correlation coefficients of school professionals with school board members' attitude was .14 and with parents' attitude was .03. Schools in which school professionals are favorable may or may not be in districts with favorable parents or board members.

Table VII-2 also supports the fifth hypothesis. The variable "Financial Resources Available for Innovation" (board members' perception) is significantly related to availability (r = .48). For both parents and board members, local financial resources is an important force. This finding supports the conclusion drawn by Carlson, who says "A high degree of relationship has been found between the financial resources of a school system and its innovativeness."* He notes that evidence is especially noticeable in wealthy communities. The present study extends his statement to include the 26 inadequately financed rural upper-New York school districts.

TABLE VII–2.

Relation of Community Forces (School Board Members) to Relative Standing of Schools on Two Innovation Criteria

	Board Members (r survey items vs. criteria)	
	Avail. (Post)	Usage (Post)
1. Attitude toward Modernization	.09	.22
2. Community Desire for Quality (Pre & Post)	.31 & .09	.25 & .18
3. Perception of Community Acceptance of New (Pre & Post)	.46*	.47*
4. Financial Resources of District	.48*	.26
5. Satisfaction with School (Post)	.22	.32
6. Maturity of Board:		
a. Years on Board	.33	.38*
b. Age	.42*	.28
7. Socio-Economic Level:		
a. Years of Schooling (Pre)	.48*	.31
b. Yearly Income	.50*	.32

*An r of .38 or better is needed for significance at the .05 level.

Table VII-2 supports the hypothesis that the maturity of the board, as measured by age and years of service of the members, is significantly related to availability and usage (r's = .38 and .42). It also supports the hypothesis that the socio-economic status of board members (years of schooling and income) is significantly related to availability of innovations (r = .48 and .50) Factor analysis shows that board member income is related to local financial resources — see hypothesis 5.)

Conclusions

1. Board members' attitude toward modernization are not significantly related to the criteria.
2. Their attitude toward modernization is not the center of a chain of attitudes and actions.
3. Their perception of the community acceptance of innovations is significantly related to two of the criteria — availability and usage of innovations in the school.
4. Furthermore, this perception is the center of a chain of events. It influences the board member's own attitude and his view that the school is responsive to the community's attitude. (For further discussion, see previous pages.)

*Richard O. Carlson, et al, *Change Processes in the Public Schools,* Center for the Advanced Study of Educational Administration, University of Oregon Press, Eugene, 1965, P. 60.

5. For both board members and parents, the adequacy of financial resources of the district is an important force making for differences in availability of innovations among the schools.

Ancillary Conclusions

6. Contrary to common belief, school districts with younger, newer board members do not produce more innovative schools. Schools with older members on the board, with more years of service, were higher in availability and usage of innovations.

7. Schools whose board members had a higher socio-economic level of education and income tended to have more innovations available. The more highly educated members seem to be of more help in implementing change.

The Kettering-Colgate Project was a school and community force.

CHAPTER 8
SCHOOL FORCES

Influence of Professional Staff

Theory. Doll says "Most of these forces and agencies (for curriculum improvement) exist within the school system. Always they include alert superintendents, curriculum committees, principals who want to see their schools move forward —. In addition, each school is likely to have its unofficial or emergent leaders who stimulate the personnel to improve their positions."* He goes on to say that classroom teachers or faculty largely determine the curriculum. Some writers disagree and maintain that while this may be true for universitites, in the public schools the teachers look to the administrator to initiate or advocate change.

Brickell says, "New types of instructional programs are introduced by administrators. Contrary to general opinion, teachers are not change agents for instructional innovations of major scope." The reference is not to changes in classroom practice but to new types of instructional programs that involve several teachers. "The control center of the institution, as schools are managed today, is the administrator. He may not be — and frequently is not — the original source of interest in a new program, but unless he gives attention to it and promotes its use, it will not come into being."

Hypothesis: To what extent does the evidence support and expand these two statements? In this study, the experimental variable (innovation) was introduced by the innovating teacher with the approval of the administration. Some experimental schools progressed more than others with respect to the criteria. What school forces were at work to bring about the differences? Several types of forces were analyzed:

1. Attitudes and actions of the classroom teachers, such as knowledge about innovations, attitude toward rapidity of change, and the teacher's own attitude toward innovations.
2. Administrative leadership in introducing innovations.
3. The innovative teacher's leadership and efforts at diffusion. (See Chapter 5 for the latter.)
4. Forces within the system, such as the health or climate of the school as indicated by the trust, openness and adaptability of the staff, and communication within the school and to the outside.

EXHIBIT VIII:

INVENTORY OF EDUCATIONAL PRACTICES (IEP): Definitions and Sample Items Assessing School Forces such as Faculty Attitudes, Actions and Social Climate.

School Forces
    A. Variables (Attitudes and Actions):
        1. Knowledge about innovations.
            a. Compared to other teachers in your school, where do you rank yourself in terms of the information that you possess about innovations?

---

*Ronald C. Doll, *Curriculum Improvement: Decision-Making and Process,* Allyn and Bacon, Inc., Boston, 1964, p. 189.

A. Very informed
B. Quite informed
C. About equally informed and equally uninformed
D. Quite uninformed
E. Very uninformed

2. Attitude toward Rapidity of Change.
    a. In general which rate of educational change do you prefer?
       A. Very rapid
       B. Quite rapid
       C. Moderately rapid
       D. Quite gradual
       E. Very gradual

3. Own attitude toward innovation.
    a. Which category best describes your own attitude toward the introduction of new ideas and techniques at the secondary school level?
       A. Very favorable
       B. Quite favorable
       C. About equally favorable and unfavorable
       D. Quite unfavorable
       E. Very unfavorable

4. Personal Use of Innovations.
    a. How much use do you personally make of any curricular or technological innovation in your present position?
       A. A great deal
       B. Considerable
       C. Moderate
       D. Slight
       E. None

5. Involvement in Innovation.
    a. If you had an opportunity to introduce an innovation and participate in a university-sponsored, in-service training program next year, would you like to do so?
       A. Most definitely yes
       B. Probably yes
       C. Undecided
       D. Probably no
       E. Definitely no

6. Administrative and Faculty Leadership in Determining which Innovations are Introduced.
    a. In general how much influence do you feel the following groups of professionals have in determining which innovations are introduced into your school?

	A great deal	Considerable	Moderate	Slight	None
Administrators	(A)	(B)	(C)	(D)	(E)
Faculty in the school	(A)	(B)	(C)	(D)	(E)
Innovative Teachers	(A)	(B)	(C)	(D)	(E)

7. Health of the System (See last part of chapter for definition and illustrations).
    a. Trust
    b. Openness
    c. Adaptability

With respect to the four types of forces, six hypotheses were formulated. The first three were chains of actions and attitudes that might have occurred within each school, as described in a previous chapter. (Chapter 6). The second three are single forces or chains of forces. It was hypothesized that the following forces within the school were related to each other and to the criteria:

1. The degree of a faculty member's knowledge about innovations and his personnal use of innovations
2. His general attitude toward validity of change, his attitude toward educational innovations and willingness to participate in innovative projects
3. The innovative teacher's leadership and his own attitude toward innovations
4. Administrative leadership in introducing innovations
5. The climate of the staff as measured by trust, opinions and adaptability
6. The effectiveness of school originated communications, within the school and to the community.

Two other school forces have been and will be discussed. The influence of diffusion by innovating teachers has been discussed in Chapter 5 under the "ripple" approach. Treated in Chapter 9, will be knowledge about the Kettering Project itself as a force.

Procedure. To test these hypotheses, six items were written for from the Inventory of Educational Practices (IEP) and administered to all the professional school personnel in all experimental schools during the pre- and post-surveys. (See Exhibit VIII-1) Correlation coefficients were then calculated between all items and between the items and each of the six criteria to determine whether there was a chain of events for individual school personnel and whether schools standing higher on the chain were higher with respect to the criteria.

Evidence and Discussion

Knowledge and Use. We have proceeded on the assumption that one of the reasons some schools did not modernize was that the faculty lacked knowledge, training and confidence in using the new procedures. For example, we deliberately arranged effective training opportunities for the innovating teachers. If the assumption is correct, this study should find that teachers who have more knowledge about innovations use them more. Schools that have more knowledgeable staff members in this respect should progress more on the criteria. (The first hypothesis) Figure IX-2 demonstrates that this is true to a moderate extent. Knowledge about innovations is significantly related to personal use of innovations $(r = .39)$. The latter variable in turn is related to the criterion faculty attitude $(.59)$, to usage $(.48)$, but not to gain. This suggests that although with faculty, knowledge and personal use is a force, the knowledge was not necessarily due to this project. To interpret the meaning of the size of the correlation coefficient, see Table V-2.

| | Effect on School |
| | (Pearson's r with criteria*) |

Variables

1. Knowledge about Innovations

    ↓↑   .39

    Personal Use of Innovations ⟶

| Attitude | (.59) |
| Usage | (.48) |

FIGURE VIII-1. Staff Knowledgeability and Use of Innovations

Figure VIII-1 should be read as follows: Knowledge about innovations is related to personal use of innovation by the teacher and the latter is significantly related to (makes a difference in) attitude and usage in the school as a whole. Knowledge about innovations by itself is not related to the criteria.

Attitude and Involvement. Faculty members' own attitude toward innovation (self-report item) is definitely related to the criteria faculty attitude in the school ($r = .70$) and to gain in faculty attitude during the experiment ($r = .50$). This gain can be attributed to the intervention of the project. It seems to have been limited to gain in attitude and not carried over into actual usage. The teacher's own attitude toward educational innovation seems to be related to whether he has a favorable attitude toward rapidity of change ($r = .53$), and desire to participate in a University-sponsored project next year ($r = .55$).

Attitude toward Rapidity of Change

↓↑   .53

Attitude toward Innovations ⟶

↓↑   .55

Willingness to Participate in a new Innovative Project

| Attitude | (.70) |
| Gain in Attitude | (.50) |

FIGURE VIII-2. Chains of Teacher Attitudes and Involvement in Innovation

Innovative Teacher Leadership. Innovative teacher's leadership brought about a gain in faculty attitude ($r = .53$). Word of mouth and diffusion by the innovating teacher may influence the attitude of others but not their usage of innovation. The evidence seems to support the idea advanced by Brickell, namely, that in most schools teachers must rely on the leadership and priority setting by the administrator. He has a strong influence in successfully introducing innovation, at least as schools are now organized. In some instances the faculty, innovating teachers, or students, may influence attitude change, but change in availability and usage are dependent on the administrator's initiative.

Innovative Teacher's Leadership in
Introducing Innovations

↓↑   .30

Own Attitude toward Innovations ⟶

| Attitude Gain | (.53) |
| Attitude | (.41) |

FIGURE VIII-3. Innovative Teacher Leadership and its Influence on the School.

*An r of .19 or over is needed for significance at the .05 level for r's in column 1 and of .38 or over for column 2.

Note: Figures VIII-2 to VIII-5 show data for chains of events (individual attitudes and actions) by professional school personnel (N=687) leading to school innovations (N=21).

Administrative Leadership. If the staff reported that the local administrator had considerable influence in determining which innovations were introduced in the school, that school gained more in both availability (r = .44) and usage (r = .42). It would seem, therefore, that the "administrative leadership" was a force making for change and was reinforced in this influence by the project.

| Administrator's Leadership in Introducing Innovations | → | Gain in Availability (.44) Gain in Usage (.42) |

FIGURE VIII-4. Administrative Leadership as Viewed by Teachers

Implications. In introducing new practices into a school, a gain in actual availability and usage of innovations results, if the faculty feel that the administration is influential in determining which innovations are introduced. Administrative leadership seems to be an important force. This may seem, as Brickell suggested, that to modernize a school, an innovative administration is essential and that to be successful, it is necessary that the administration be convinced of the value of the new types of practices.

Communication. The effectiveness of communication within the school and to the community seem to be fairly closely related to each other. A school that successfully disseminates information about innovation in one respect, seems to do it well in the other. However, such communication was not found to have any significant impact on the criteria. This finding is contrary to accepted theory. Attention should be called to the fact that only one aspect of communication was measured; namely, school-originated information about innovation. Later it will be seen that information about the Kettering Project may have had more influence.

Communication of Information within School	Gain in Attitude (.24)
↓↑ .67	and (.30)
Communication to Community (about Innovations)	(Not significant)

FIGURE VIII-5. The influence of School-Originated Communication of Information on Innovativeness.

Openness, Trust and Adaptability. The literature suggests that staff openness, trust and adaptability are related to innovativeness in a system. Hilfiker tested the hypothesis that there was a significant relationship existing among these three variables, and innovations in eight school systems. He found a significant relationship for the first two, but not for adaptiveness. Others have discussed the relationship of innovativeness and adaptiveness to organizational health. Health was thought to be a necessary ingredient of innovation.

To test the hypothesis that staff openness, trust and adaptiveness are related to school innovativeness, (see previous hypothesis 5), ten of the fourteen items from Hilfiker's scale were administered to the professional staff in the 26 experimental schools.* (See Appendix B, for items and scoring procedure.) Staff members first

---

*Leo R. Hilfiker, *The Relationship of School System Innovativeness to Selected Dimensions of Interpersonal Behavior in Eight School Systems,* Wisconsin Research and Development Center for Cognitive Learning, The University of Wisconsin, Madison, Wisconsin, January 1969.

indicated their perception of other's feelings regarding the items, and then their own feelings. Hilfiker used only the individual respondents' own feelings. The present study does likewise. As in the COPED study, only the self-perception results are reported in Table VIII-1.

The COPED instrument was designed to measure individually perceived standards which govern interpersonal relations with others in an organizational setting. It defined the three variables, as follows: (See Appendix B for complete instrument.)

1. "Openness — the degree to which an individual perceives interpersonal relationships as being characterized by ready accessibility, cooperative attitude, tolerance of internal change and permissiveness of diversity in social situations."
    Sample item: "Keep your real thoughts and reactions to yourself, by and large." (Negative item)
2. "Trust — the degree to which an individual perceives interpersonal relationships as characterized by an assured reliance or confident dependence upon the character, ability, or truthfulness of others."
    Sample item: "Be skeptical about things as a rule." (Negative item)
3. "Adaptiveness — the degree to which an individual perceives interpersonal relationships as characterized by a ready capability for modification or changes in social conditions, ways, or environments."
    Sample item: "Try out new ways in doing things in one's work."

Table VIII-1, Column 1, shows that in the present study, all three variables are related to school gains in faculty attitude toward innovation, but not to gain in school level of usage. For the former the three correlation coefficients were .49, .60 and .51, respectively. (.38 needed at the .05 level.) The correlations with usage gain did not differ significantly from zero.

Table VIII-1. The Relation of Trust, Openness, and Adaptability to School Gain in the Criteria

COPED Variable	Attitude Gain	Usage Gain
Openness	.49	−.18
Trust	.60	−.24
Adaptability	.51	−.01

Conclusions

1. Faculty member knowledge about innovations is related to the extent he personally uses them and this in turn is significantly related to attitude and usage in the school, but not to availability or gain on the criteria.
2. A teacher's attitude toward rapidity of change in general is related to his own attitude toward the effectiveness of innovation and to his willingness to participate in a University-sponsored project the next year. His own attitude is the center of the sequence in that it is the only one of the three variables significantly related to the criteria, attitude and gain in attitude. His attitude had its influence on gain in school attitude during the experiment but stopped there. It did not influence usage.
3. Administrative influence in introducing innovations is the major school force apparently related to gain on actual availability and urge in the schools. The gain can be attributed to the influence of the experimental variable introduced by this project.

4. "Innovative teacher" knowledge is related to his own attitude and again related only to two criteria, faculty attitude and gain in attitude.
5. Effectiveness of communication of school-originated information about innovations within the school and to the community are related to each other, but apparently are not related to any of the criteria.
6. The health of the system as measured by the trust, openness and adaptability of the staff is related to gain in faculty attitude only.

Implications

Faculty attitude toward a new practice will be more favorable in those schools in which the faculty are more knowledgeable about innovations in general, and personally use them. Perhaps this is because they feel more comfortable and less threatened by the change if they are already trying new things.

Also, the gain in staff attitude toward innovation will be more rapid in those schools whose faculty have a favorable attitude and express greater willingness to participate in new University-sponsored projects.

It would seem, therefore, that in introducing a new process, the faculty should be made as knowledgeable as possible about innovations, either through a "ripple" approach and its accompanying diffusion by the leadership of such a person as the Innovating Teacher; or through some equivalent process, such as visitations to other projects. School originated communications alone do not seem to have much influence. The preceding steps may develop a more favorable faculty attitude toward a new practice.

Another influence on gain in faculty attitude toward change is the climate of the system, or its unwritten norms of interpersonal relationships with respect to trust, openness and adaptability. This may mean that if a new practice is to be favorably accepted by the faculty and the faculty is to gain in their attitude toward change and not have a "set-back", there should be an effort by all of the staff, including administrators, to increase the support of trust and openness and reduce the friction within the system. Administrators and department heads have many ways of attacking this problem. These are beyond the scope of this study, but are treated elsewhere.*

---

*Andrew W. Halpin, "Theory and Research in Administration," Chapter 4, *The Organizational Climate of Schools,* The Macmillan Company, 1966.

CHAPTER 9

COMMUNICATION AND KNOWLEDGE ABOUT THE KETTERING—COLGATE PROJECT AS A FORCE IN THE SCHOOL AND COMMUNITY

Knowledge About and Influence of the Project

Board and Parent Knowledge. Board members and parents were asked the same survey questions in 1970: "How much do you know about the innovation supported by the Kettering-Colgate Project at your secondary school?"

Hypothesis. Schools which gained most in the criteria had board members and parents who were better informed about the Project. In other words, successful diffusion of information about the Project led to greater gain in attitude, availability or usage in the school. Table IX-1 presents the evidence.

Discussion of the Evidence. Schools whose board members reported that they were well informed about the local Kettering-Colgate Project gained more in availability of innovations (as reported by the faculty ($r = .44$). The relationship between being well informed about the Kettering-Colgate Project and gain in availability of innovations in the local secondary school seems logical. Board members do vote for or against the support that makes more innovations available. Also logical is the finding that the extent to which parents were well informed about the project seemed to have no significant relationship to the criteria.

Faculty Knowledge. School professionals were asked the question "How much influence has the Kettering-Colgate Project had on innovations within your school?"

Hypothesis. Schools whose professionals reported more influence by the Kettering-Colgate Project tended to have gained most on the criteria.

Discussion of Evidence. If the faculty members of a school reported that the Kettering-Colgate Project had considerable influence, the school tended to make a significant gain in usage (as rated by outside experts, $r = .43$). This gain may have been related to attempts at diffusion of a local project by the innovating teacher. The finding tended to reinforce a conclusion discussed earlier (Chapter 5); namely, that dissemination by the innovating teacher influenced the usage level of innovation in the school.

TABLE IX-1. The Kettering-Colgate Project as a School and Community Force Leading to Change in the Schools

Variables	Effect on School Pearson's r =
1. Amount of Knowledge about the Kettering-Colgate Project (by Board Members) vs. School Gain in Availability of Innovations	.44*
2. Amount of knowledge about the Kettering-Colgate Project (by Parents) vs. Criteria	No significant change
3. Belief that Kettering-Colgate Project has considerable influence (by School Professionals) vs. School Gain in Usage of Innovations	.43

*An r of .38 is needed for significance at the .05 level.

Conclusions

1. Schools whose board members reported they were well informed about the local Kettering-Colgate Project, gained more in availability of innovations.
2. School districts in which parents were well-informed about the Kettering-Colgate Project did not gain more on the criteria than schools in which parents were less well informed. It would seem that parents have less direct influence on availability of innovations, than do board members.
3. Those schools whose teachers reported that the Kettering-Colgate Project had considerable influence on innovation, gained more usage than did schools that reported less influence. This conclusion may support the finding that the amount of diffusion by the innovating teacher is related to gain in usage.

Communication, Parents and Board Members

The Influence of Brochures. Two printed brochures, attractively illustrated with photographs, were circulated to samplings of parents and board members. The samples were controlled so that the impact of the brochures could be assessed. At the time of publication, each set of brochures was mailed to a random sampling of approximately 1000 parents and school board members. A sampling, approximately equal in size, received no brochures

Hypothesis. (1) There will be a significant difference between the groups receiving and not receiving the brochure, in the amount of information about innovation in the local school. (2) There will be a significant difference between the two samples in the amount of information they report they have about the Kettering Colgate Project.

Discussion of Evidence. The data for board members were separated from those for parents. Thus, two conclusions can be drawn about each of the hypotheses — one for parents and one for board members. Simple analyses of variance techniques were employed to test the differences. Table IX-2 shows the results. The sets of figures in the first row showed that receiving the brochure did not help the board members know more about innovation in their school (F = .25) but it did increase their information about the Kettering-Colgate Project (F = 14.9). They already had considerable knowledge about their local school innovations (Mean = 3.7). For parents, (second row of figures), those receiving the brochure tended to increase their knowledge about innovation in the local school (F = 21.25) and their knowledge about the Kettering-Colgate Project (F = 62.7). The amount of information reported by parents was less than that reported by board members, and especially so for parents who did not receive the brochure. (The mean amount of information on the Kettering Project for parents who did not receive the brochure was 1.52 compared to 3.37 for board members who did.)

TABLE IX-2. Knowledge about Innovations in the Local Secondary School and about the Kettering Project

Group	How much do you know about innovations in the local secondary school?			How much do you know about innovations supported by the Kettering-Colgate Project?	
	N	Mean	F	Mean	F
Board Members:					
Received the brochures	90	3.68	.25	3.37	14.89*
Did not receive the brochures	32	3.75		2.26	
Parents:					
Received the brochures	299	2.96	21.25*	2.39	162.67*
Did not receive the brochures	653	2.61		1.52	

*Significant at the .05 level.

Implications. The brochures were an effective means of communication to board members and parents, but especially to parents. For board members, brochures were effective in providing specific information about the Kettering-Colgate Project. However, the boards already had a considerable amount of knowledge about innovations in general in their local schools. (Mean = 3.9)

Communication, School Professionals and the Brochures

School Professionals Another experimental design was arranged to test the influence of the brochure on school professionals. Brochures were mailed to individuals in randomly selected schools: (1) to all of the professionals in half the experimental schools; (2) to half the professionals in the remaining experimental schools; (3) to half of the professionals in half the control schools and to none of the professionals in the remaining control schools. Respondees replied to the first question, "How much do you know about the innovations supported by the Kettering-Colgate Project at your secondary school?" and to a new question "How much has receiving the brochure influenced your attitude toward innovation?"

Hypothesis. (1) Receiving the brochure was related to how much professional staff members knew about the innovations supported by the Kettering-Colgate Project in their school. (2) Receiving the brochure influenced the professional staff's attitude toward innovation.

Discussion of Evidence. Table IX-3 shows that both experimental hypotheses must be rejected. Receiving the brochure had little influence on professional staff knowledge about the Kettering-Colgate Project or on attitude toward innovation. This is quite the contrary to the findings with respect to school board members and parents.

Section A of the table shows that in the experimental schools there was no significant difference between the average amount of knowledge concerning the Kettering-Colgate Project for the group in which all received the brochures (mean = 2.88) and the group in which only half received it (mean = 3.00). Likewise, there was no difference between the control group in which one half received the brochure (mean = 2.02) and the one in which no professionals received it. The only significant difference was between all of the experimental group and all of the control group. The experimental group knew more about the project (mean = 2.95) than the control group (mean = 1.95), brochure or no brochure. This is understandable since the action phase of the project was in the experimental schools.

Section B of Table IX-3 shows that all of the sub-group means are approximately equal (2.4 to 2.5), regardless of whether all received the brochure, one-half received the brochure, none received it; or whether they were in the experimental or control group. There was no difference in the amount that the brochure influenced their attitudes. If the brochures had a significant influence on school professionals, we would have expected to find that the size of the group means increased in proportion to the number of its members who received the brochure.

Relative Communication Power of the Brochure

Attached to the brochures was a return postcard asking which procedures helped the recipient learn most about the new practices in their secondary school. There were 254 replies received. Of the ten listed sources of information, the five receiving the most first choices were: (1) word of mouth; (2) bulletins and newsletters; (3) local school functions; (4) books and periodicals, and (5) newspapers. Choice number two — bulletins and newsletters was interpreted as being similar to the brochures in this study. However, the implication needs to be tempered with the reminder that those who returned the card were the ones most influenced by the brochures.

The extent of communication power of a single brochure is indicated by the answers to the question, "With how many adults do you estimate you will discuss this bulletin?" The average number was over five. Thus, for the 254 respondees, the communication power of a single brochure may be five times as great as expected. One administrator whose school was not in the Project, wrote on the card under Comments, "We are reinforced in our innovative efforts by this material. We'd like to join the Project, if possible."

Conclusions

1. Receiving the brochures did not help board members know what was going on in the way of innovation in their local secondary schools, but it did help in knowing more about the innovations supported by the Kettering-Colgate Project.
2. There was significant difference in favor of parents who did, as opposed to those who did not receive the brochure, with respect to how much they knew about innovation in the local secondary school in general and about the innovations supported by the Kettering-Colgate Project in particular.
3. Receiving the brochures did not influence how much the professional staff knew about the Kettering-Colgate Project, or their attitudes toward innovation. Being in an experimental school, rather then in a control school, did influence the professional staff, but the brochures did not.

Comments

Communication about a project to board members, but not to parents, seems to be important in making gains in availability. For board members, receiving the brochures helped them know about a specific project, but they already seemed well informed in general about innovations in their schools. For parents, receiving the brochures had considerable impact both on their knowledge about innovations in the school and especially about their knowledge of the specific Kettering-Colgate Project. For professional staff members in the experimental schools, knowledge about the Kettering-Colgate Project seemed to be an ingredient for gain in actual usage of innovations. Thus, it would seem that dissemination of the Kettering-Colgate Project was important to usage. Receiving the brochures seemed not to be effective for the professional staff. Dissemination by the innovating teacher ("word of mouth") was. (See Chapter 5.) The brochure was written with the layman in mind.

TABLE IX-3. The Influence of the Brochures on Professional Staff.

A. Knowledge about the Kettering-Colgate Project by Professional Staff:

Sub-Group:		N	Mean
1.	Experimental schools (all staff received brochures)	240	2.88
2.	Experimental schools (one-half staff received brochures)	380	3.00
3.	Control schools (one-half staff received brochures)	116	2.04
4.	Control schools (none of staff received brochures)	106	1.89

F (1 vs 2) = 2.48 F (2 vs 3) = 95.53*

B. Extent that Attitude Toward Innovation was influenced by the Brochures.

Sub-Group:	N	Mean
1. Experimental Schools (all staff received brochures)	240	2.41
2. Experimental Schools (one-half staff received brochures)	346	2.54
3. Control Schools (one-half staff received brochures)	84	2.46
4. Control Schools (none of staff received brochures)	53	2.43

$$F (2 \text{ vs } 3) = .40 \qquad F (3 \text{ vs } 4) = .03$$

The two brochures influenced parents but not school professionals.

---

*Significant at the .05 level.

CHAPTER 10
EFFECT OF THE PROJECT ON STUDENTS

Student Participation

The IET. One objective of the Project was to determine the impact of the effective introduction of innovation (and its "ripple" effect throughout the school) on the students. To assess this, two measures were selected: the Inventory of Educational Techniques, and the Inventory of Educational Opinions.

The first, Inventory of Educational Techniques, was a newly-constructed twenty-six item instrument, which measured three variables:

1. Use of Media, or the extent to which a student was involved with any of twelve new technologies in his studies for a given week in 1968 and again in 1970.
2. Use of New Instructional Procedures, or the extent to which the student's instruction in school encompassed team teaching, differential grouping (large group — small group), new electives, independent study, and use of a learning center during the same weeks.
3. Direct Student Participation, or whether the student prepared materials to use with equipment, and used equipment himself during these weeks.

Procedure. The instrument was administered to 1053 pupils who were asked to recall which activities had taken place during the week. The time intervals selected in which to obtain a representative sample were two one-week periods; the first in 1968 (pre-test) and again in February 1970 (post-test). The three variables were then correlated with each of the six criteria to determine whether those experimental schools which were high on the criteria had more impact on the nature of the instruction which the student received, than did the low schools. (Pearson r's)

Evidence and Discussion. Table X-1 shows that availability of innovations (rater's estimate) in a school was significantly correlated with a gain on all three variables. Availability (Post) made it possible for the pupils to increase their participation significantly. The correlation coefficients for the three variables and total, $(6 - 9)$, with the post-availability criterion were .40, .49, .37, and .50, respectively (an r of .38 is needed for significance at the .05 level). No relationship was found with gain in Availability or with any of the other four criteria.

TABLE X-1. Relationship of the Inventory of Technique Variables, Post and Gain (Pupil Participation) to the Two Criteria — Post-Availability and Gain in Availability of Innovations.

I.E.T. Variable	Post-Availability (r)	Availability Gain (r)
Post (1) Media	.36	.20
Post (2) New Instructional Procedures	.48	-.03
Post (3) Direct Student Participation	.26	.04
Post (4) Total	.38	.15
Gain (6) Media	.40	.20
Gain (7) New Instructional Procedures	.49	.02
Gain (8) Direct Student Participation	.37	.08
Gain (9) Total	.50	.18

The fact that student gain on the IET variables was not related to school gain in availability suggests that it was the level of availability of innovations that led to increased student participation and not necessarily gain in availability that took place during the two years of the experiment.

One set of forces that has not been investigated is student power. After the present research study was initiated, students gained a stronger role in governance. At the university level, they are now voting members on university policy-making councils and commissions. Student influence at the secondary school level is powerful but seems to be extended in different ways. According to school administrators, student influence may be either indirect or direct. In some urban districts, students indirectly influence change by demonstrating their alienation through vandalism, absenteeism and under-achievement. Indirectly this causes the professional staff to bring about change. Some schools treat responsible students as equals and develop a school-wide plan for student participation in the decision-making process with respect to vital school policy. Future studies of the forces making for change will need to consider student power. This research project studied the effect of the innovations on the student, but did not study his impact on the innovations process.

Conclusion. Experimental schools with more innovations available (rater's judgment) had greater impact on student participation in innovative experiences (as reported by the pupils) than did the other experimental schools.

Effect of the Project on Dynamics of Teaching Learning Process

The IEO. The second measure of the effect of the project on students, the Inventory of Educational Opinions, was developed by Walberg. It contained fourteen sets of variables of four items each. They are listed in Table X-2. Each item asked the student to respond to a statement describing dynamic aspects in all of his classes. The instrument seems to be well-constructed. Factor analysis confirmed the fact that twelve of the fourteen variables were "unique". It was administered to 988 students in 1968 and again to the same students two years later in 1970. The fourteen variables were then correlated with six criteria to determine whether the schools who rated high in the criterion gained more on the fourteen IEO variables, than schools who rated low. (Pearson r's)

Discussion. Table X-2 shows that gain in school attitude (rater's estimate) toward innovations is positively related to two of the IEO variables: Lack of Friction ($r = .56$) and Goal Direction ($r = .38$). This suggests that students in schools whose faculties gain more in attitude toward innovations: (1) Reduce the bad feelings that interfere with classroom activites, and their disrespect for other students (Lack of Friction); and (2) Gain a better understanding of what their classes are supposed to accomplish (Goal Direction). On the other hand, the relationship with informality is negative ($r = -.57$). This indicates that students in schools whose faculties gain a more favorable attitude toward innovations, perceive their classroom organization to be less casual and to have more than the usual rules to follow. Perhaps this evidence is saying that as the teachers become more favorable toward arranging independent study, differential scheduling and toward other such innovations, they discover that they must plan more carefully, and provide more guidelines, more clearly defined goals, and more pre-planned individual learning activities. Pupils may see these changes as an increase in formality.

Gain in school usage (rater's estimate) is related to one IEO variable — Appropriate Difficulty ($r = .41$). The more a school gained in sophisticated use of innovations, the more the students perceived their classroom activities to be paced at an appropriate level of difficulty. For example, students at different levels of achievement have time to finish their work. (See Table X-2, column two.)

TABLE X-2. The Relationship of 14 I.E.O. Classroom Climate Variables to the Gain of Schools on Two Criteria (N=26 schools, 98 pupils)

Variable	School Attitude Gain (r)*	School Usage Gain (r)
1. Intimacy	.08	.07
2. Lack of Friction	.56	-.21
3. Non-Cliquishness	.12	-.05
4. Non-Apathy	.14	-.02
5. Lack of Favoritism	-.04	-.03
6. Informality	-.57	.36
7. Satisfaction	.31	-.22
8. Appropriate Speed	.21	.03
9. Appropriate Difficulty	-.18	.41
10. Goal Direction	.38	-.23
11. Democracy	-.04	.26
12. Organization	.37	-.15
13. Diversity	.34	-.18
14. Physical Environment (Space)	-.36	.29

*A Pearson's r of .38 is needed for significance at the .05 level.

CHAPTER 11
COMPARATIVE STUDY OF INNOVATION AND LEADERSHIP
PATTERNS AT TWO HIGH SCHOOLS*

The purpose of this part of the study was to provide some insight into the dynamics of innovations through the comparative study of two high schools. The schools were selected by the staff of the Kettering-Colgate Project. The staff judgment was that the two schools were comparable in terms of size, budget, physical facility, but divergent in terms of acceptance and introduction of innovative educational techniques. One of the schools, which shall be called School A, tended to be more receptive to change; while the other school, which shall be called School B, tended to be indifferent toward the introduction of new practices.

Study of Schools A and B

Procedure. The study proceeded on the basis of personal interviews with the top administrative personnel and the teaching staff. A random sample of fifteen teachers was drawn for each school and interviews were conducted by means of an interview schedule. Due to the small sample of respondents and the non-parametric data, the analysis is represented by percentage findings.

Patterns of Leadership in Two Schools The administration of School A exerts an active leadership in the introduction of new educational directions. The form of leadership is forceful and not authoritarian. Subordinates are consulted concerning new school policy and the faculty vote on the proposed changes. The leadership provides an environment for innovation. Ideologically, the administration makes it clear what it considers the desirable direction to be. It does this in the initial placement interviews, encourages the adoption of innovations during classroom visits, and prepares the teachers as much as possible for major changes.

School B offers a contrasting pattern of leadership. Although the administration is responsible for the running of the school, no initiative is taken for changes in the general philosophy of the organization. The administration does not take a strong ideological stance on educational change. It neither resists nor encourages change. The leadership takes up a non-directive approach, leaving initiative for change as well as critical decisions affecting the organization as a whole for the teaching faculty to decide.

In the survey, leadership patterns were examined in terms (1) of the way in which teachers perceived the relative influence of themselves and the administration in decision-making; (2) the basis for power and authority; and (3) the evaluation of the organization.

Decision-Making Pattern. Table XI-1 compares the perception of influence by the Faculty of the Schools A and B.

TABLE XI-1. Perception of Influence in Two Schools**

Type of Influence Pattern	School % A	School % B
High Administration High Teacher	67% (10)	27% (04)
High Administration Low Teacher	33% (05)	00% (00)

---

*Prepared by Raymond E. Ries, Professor of Sociology and E. Howard Borck, Instructor in Sociology, Colgate University, for this aspect of the study.
**Interview data Chi Square = 14.4, significant at the .05 level.

(TABLE XI-1. continued)

Type of Influence Pattern	School % A	School % B
Low Administration High Teacher	00% (00)	67% (10)
Low Administration Low Teacher	00% (00)	06% (01)
	100% (15)	100% (15)

Over two-thirds of the faculty of the School B report a low administration and high teacher influence in decision-making. In contrast, two-thirds of the School A faculty report high influence for both faculty and administration. All of the respondents at School A report high administrative influence, while 94 percent of the School B respondents report high teacher influence.

Power and Authority. The respondents were asked to examine the basis for administrative authority (Table XI-2).

TABLE XI-2. Perceptions of the Basis of Administrative Authority

At Schools A and B*

Basis of Power	School A % rating as first, first or second		School B % rating as first, first or second	
Admiration	07% (01)	36% (05)	00% (00)	13% (02)
Competence	64% (09)	78% (11)	33% (05)	60% (09)
Positive Rewards	00% (00)	14% (03)	07% (01)	27% (04)
Negative Rewards	00% (00)	21% (03)	07% (01)	20% (03)
Legitimacy	29% (04)	43% (06)	53% (08)	80% (12)
Other	08% (01)	08% (01)	00% (00)	00% (00)
	100% (15)		100% (15)	

Administrative authority is generally perceived at School B to be based on the legitimate authority of the office; whereas at School A, authority is grounded in what the teachers perceive as the competence of the administrators. Thus the high degree of administrative influence perceived at School A is associated with their competence; the high teacher influence reported at School B with the more formal basis for administrative authority.

This suggests that an administration which gives little direction in defining the goals of the school is given a formal basis of authority. The degree of teacher influence may be less important than the need for competent direction.

We have described the different leadership aspects at schools A and B. The following summary may clarify our argument.

School A	School B
1. High perceived administrative and teacher influence.	1. Low perceived administrative influence. High perceived teacher influence.
2. Shared responsibility for leadership and decisions.	2. Responsibility for leadership assumed by employees.

---

*Objective data gathered from an instrument prepared by the authors. Colgate University, 1971. Chi Square = 6.5, significant at the .05 level.

School A (continued)
School A (continued)

3. Firm, directive leadership
4. Administrative encouragement and initiation of changes and innovations
5. Power and authority generally based on competence and respect of judgment

School B (continued)

3. Lack of firm, directive leadership
4. Status-quo policy of administration
5. Power and authority generally based on legitimacy

Evaluation of the System. Given these differences between the high schools, our next task is to examine our main dependent measure: evaluation of the school system by employees. This evaluation index consists of ten factors measured independently: Trustfulness, Creativity, Sensitivity, Genuineness, Facing Problems, Concern, Credibility, Development, Flexibility and Competence. This evaluative measure has been linked with overall morale and job satisfaction. Studies suggest that the more a person perceives that he has influence in the system, the more positively he will evaluate the system.

If this latter hypothesis is confirmed, we should find higher evaluations of the system at School B since nearly all of the respondents reported high influence.

TABLE XI-3. Evaluations by Schools A and B*

Evaluative Factor	School A Mean Score	School B Mean Score	Mean Difference
Trustfulness	1.9	2.0	.1
Creativity	1.8	2.9	1.1**
Sensitivity	2.1	2.6	.5
Genuineness	2.0	2.4	.4
Facing Problems	1.8	3.2	1.4**
Concern	1.8	2.3	.5
Credibility	2.0	2.2	.2
Development	1.6	2.7	1.1**
Flexibility	1.8	2.4	.6
Competence	1.7	2.2	.5
Sum mean: 1.86	Sum mean: 2.50	Sum mean diff.: .64**

Table XI-3 shows the comparative semantic differential means for each evaluative criterion. A score of 1 is the highest positive evaluation. There is an overall difference between the two schools on evaluation. In all ten categories, School A is evaluated higher than School B. The greatest difference on items appears with Creativity, Facing Problems, and Development; these items are closely related to changes and innovations.

Discussion and Conclusions. The analysis reveals that the leadership and authority patterns at School A lead to higher evaluation of the system by the workers; this leads to high morale and satisfaction and is organizationally desirable. This finding holds regardless of whether the subordinates perceive high influence. Even though more of the respondents at School B perceived high teacher influence, lower

*Data were gathered using an interview instrument prepared by the authors, "Evaluation of the School System", Colgate University, 1970.
**Significant at the .05 level (t's = 4.9, 4.8, 3.4 and 2.9 respectively).

evaluations of the system are reported. This finding suggests that the more effective system operates under strong, initiating leadership as opposed to leaving leadership to the teachers. Participation is an important element of change at School A, but this participation takes the primary form of consideration of employees, rather than a basic decision-making delegation of power. The administration at School A decides a particular direction to take and then approaches the faculty for approval.

Several teachers at School B suggested that turning to the faculty for decisions in critical areas is to "open a can of worms." Teachers are aware of the pressures and counter-pressures for change in educational circles, yet are unable or willing to provide a direction themselves. This is consistent with the more positive evaluation of School A with its highly influential and directive leadership.

M.B. Miles* has suggested that among the special features of schools as social organizations is that the goals of the schools tend to be difficult to define or measure. School personnel have no clear framework within which to evaluate their own achievement. This, along with the pressure for change, would explain the desire of teachers for an administrative leadership which addresses itself to the problems of educational goals and innovation.

An administration which exerts an active influence would, of course, need to be cognizant of countervailing pressures which its own activity might generate. Yet the data reveal that (Table XI-3) clique formation is perceived by more respondents at School B than at School A and that at both schools cliques are perceived as countervailing. It appears that cliques will develop with some countervailing tendencies regardless of type of leadership and emphasis or lack of emphasis on change and educational goals.

Summary

We have examined innovation in two high schools. One of these schools is highly innovative while the other supports a condition of status-quo. We find that the primary difference between the schools is the extent of educational direction given by the administration. The school with high innovation is characterized by an administration which actively supports educational change. In this change-oriented system, the basis of administrative authority is seen as competence, and the school is perceived by its teachers as facing problems and developing. The status-quo system has lower evaluations and the basis of administrative authority is seen as legitimacy.

It appears that an innovative climate is dependent on the type of administrative leadership in a system. Due to varied and changing educational philosophies, teachers seem to need clear educational direction and support provided by their administration. Without this direction, teachers will be unable to determine for themselves the educational philosophy of the school.

---

*M. B. Miles, quoted in "Influence and Satisfaction in Organizations: A Replication", Harvey A. Hornstein, D. M. Callahan, E. Fisch, and B. A. Benedict in *Sociology of Education,* Fall 1968, Vol. 41, No. 4, pp. 380-389.

These measures are based on a previous study:

J. G. Bachman, C. G. Smith, and J. A. Slesinger, "Control, Performance, and Satisfaction: An Analysis of Structural and Individual Effects," *Journal of Personality and Social Psychology,* Vol. 4, 1966, pp. 127-136.

Exhibit XI-1. Evaluation of the School System. (A semantic differential scale)**

What are your feelings concerning your school on the following attributes. Place a check on the line closest to how you feel your school reflects each item.

1. mistrustful ___ ___ ___ ___ ___ trustful

2. creative ___ ___ ___ ___ ___ not creative

3. insensitive ___ ___ ___ ___ ___ sensitive

4. genuine ___ ___ ___ ___ ___ phony

5. facing problems ___ ___ ___ ___ ___ avoiding problems

6. unconcerned ___ ___ ___ ___ ___ concerned

7. deceptive ___ ___ ___ ___ ___ credible

8. developing ___ ___ ___ ___ ___ not developing

9. rigid ___ ___ ___ ___ ___ flexible

10. incompetent ___ ___ ___ ___ ___ competent

**Items 2, 4, 5, 8 are scored 1, 2, 3, 4, 5. For the remaining items, the scale is reversed. The instrument was used in interview situations.

62

CHAPTER 12
SUMMARY USING MULTIPLE CORRELATION

From the beginning of this project, our intent was to determine the relative importance of school and community forces. In this summary of the relative importance of these forces, two questions are raised. (1) Which forces account for most of the difference among schools? It is possible that some forces identified in earlier chapters are so closely related to others that they really are not separate forces. Analysis might reveal there were a few major forces from one source, parents, which overshadowed the others. (2) How much of the differences among the schools can be accounted for by all of the important variables combined into a pattern of forces? It is possible that pressure exerted by school professionals, the school board, parents, and others account for nearly all the variances or very little of it. It is important to know the extent to which a school could influence the degree of its innovativeness if it could understand all of the forces identified.

Procedure.

All of the previous variables that showed promise of significantly influencing innovations in the schools were selected for a multiple correlation regression analysis. This is a technique commonly used to study the extent to which a battery of several variables predict a criterion. For example, administrative leadership may be one variable that makes for a difference in school gain in innovation. There may be other forces, such as the school's climate of trust, which also is a significant influence. The two together may account for more of the total variance among the schools than either one alone. However, if trust is a function of administrative leadership, the former will not add to the predictiveness. Use of the multiple correlation and regression technique enables one to summarize the findings by showing the extent to which all of the forces working together make for differences in innovativeness among the schools.

The first step was to select the promising variables to be included in the multiple analysis. These were entered in a step-wise regression program to determine which were most important, the second most important, and so on, until the remaining variables contributed almost nothing in addition. For each of the multiple analyses, from four to six variables appeared to be important, as shown in the accompanying tables. The second step was to decide which of the criteria we wanted to predict. Those chosen were: attitude, availability, and usage at post-survey time. They were indices of the differences among the schools at the end of the experiment. Also chosen for study, were gains in each of the three. Use of the latter identifies the forces that were most influential during the experiment.

Discussion of Evidence.

Attitude. Table XII-1 shows that four to six forces were major influences on faculty attitude. They are all internal rather than external forces, and involved the faculty rather than the administration. The most important variables for predicting the faculty attitude of a school at post-survey time were first, the spirit of openness among the faculty members.* In such schools, interpersonal relationships were characterized by ready accessability and cooperation. Also, two other aspects of school climate, trust and adaptability were predictive (See Chapter 8 for definitions.)

---

*Creativeness, problem solving, and development were assessed only for schools A and B, and could not be part of the total technique.

Second most important was the attitude of the teachers toward innovation. One would expect this variable to be important because of its similarity to the criterion. The remaining major forces were: the influence of the Innovating Teacher and diffusion to individuals by that teacher. A similar battery of variables were related to gain. They appeared in a slightly different order of importance, but most of these same ones had some influence on gain.

The size of the multiple correlation coefficients, ranging from .78 to .86, are to be interpreted in the same way as the single correlation coefficient (see Table V-2). They indicate that these forces accounted for a majority of the variance in faculty attitude among schools (60 percent to 74 percent of the variance). Similar studies are needed to confirm whether these findings can be generalized to other situations.

Availability. Seven school and community forces appear to be important influences on the availability of innovations in the schools. Three external forces were important long-range forces; two, school board influences, and one, parental influence. School board perception of (1) adequate financial resources for innovation, and (2) favorable community acceptance of innovations, were strong influences. Quite logically, parental view of the importance of program moderniza-tion was also a significant force. This reinforces the conclusion reached in earlier chapters, that parental support is important because school board members seem to relate their policy decisions to their view of community acceptance. Other factors related to availability were the extent to which teachers made personal use of innovations and the amount of diffusion by the Innovating Teacher.

Gain in availability during the project was influenced most by administrative leadership; second, by the extent of teacher usage; third, by a financial factor (socio-economic status of the board); fourth, by community acceptance of innovation as perceived by the board members; and fifth, by knowledge about the Kettering-Colgate Project among board members. There was little difference between the forces that influenced long-range availability and gain in availability during the experiment. The main difference was that the Kettering-Colgate Project was added as one of the influences. Multiple correlation coefficients shown at the bottom of Table XII-2 range from .72 to .89 and account for between 50 percent and 80 percent of the variability among the schools.

Usage. The six forces most important for Usage were similar to those for Availability, Table XII-3. Parents, board members and school personnel all seemed to have influence, although, for usage, more were internal influences. Forces in the school were: the Kettering-Colgate Project, administrative leadership, and diffusion by the Innovating Teacher. External forces were: attitude toward modernization by the parents, and maturity of board members. Community acceptance of innova-tions, as perceived by the board, appeared as an influence but most of its original relationship to the criteria had been absorbed by the third variable, parental attitude toward modernization. This tends to confirm the hypothesis that school board members were sensitive to community views and that part of the community "visible" to them was the parents.

Conclusions

1. Among the most important forces making for differences in gain in school attitude toward innovativeness were: (a) the institution climate, especially with respect to openness; (b) the influence of the Innovating Teacher; and (c) the attitude of the faculty toward change. It is interesting to note that all of these forces were internal, or within the school. A different set of forces seems to be

at work for actual Availability and Usage. Is it possible that a school's faculty could have a relatively favorable attitude toward innovation and yet not personally use innovations? If so, there either must be many frustrated teachers who want to innovate but cannot, or there are many teachers who are favorable in theory only. Personal observations in the field indicate that there is frustration brought about by the forces discussed in this report.

2. Forces influencing schools to gain most in Availability were restricted primarily to board members and faculty. Parents did not appear as an influence except indirectly through the school board. The most important forces were: (a) perceived administrative leadership; (b) personal usage of innovations by faculty members; (c) diffusion by the Innovating Teacher; and (d) selected school board forces, such as perceived financial resources, maturity, or years of service on the board, and knowledge about the Kettering-Colgate Project.

3. Forces influencing schools to gain more in Usage were the Kettering-Colgate Project, administrative leadership, and the extent to which the school staff personally used innovations. Also, not to be overlooked, was community acceptance of modernizing the school as perceived by parents.

4. The forces identified in this study accounted for a majority of the variance in innovations among schools with respect to Attitude and Availability. A sizable portion of the variance was due to unknown influences. Not as many of the forces related to Usage and usage gain were isolated. The percentage of variance accounted for these was from 42 percent to 50 percent. Measures of additional forces, beyond those developed in this project, may be needed to obtain a more complete understanding of the forces related to actual usage.

TABLE XII-1. Important School and Community Forces Influencing Differences in Attitude Toward Innovations Among the Schools

Variable (or Force)	As Perceived by	Gain in Attitude	Gain in Attitude Regressed*	Attitude Post-Survey
Trust	School Staff	.62	.40	.35**
Openness	School Staff	.50	.50	.19
Personal Attitude Toward Innovation	School Staff	.23	–	.34
Influence of Innovating Teacher	School Staff	.08	.26	.27
Adaptability	School Staff	–	.21	.16
Diffusion to Individuals	Innovating Teacher	–	.10	.08
Multiple Correlation Coefficient		.77	.86	.85

TABLE XII-2. Important School and Community Forces Influencing Differences in Availability of Innovations among the Schools.

Variable (or Force)	As Perceived by	Gain in Availability	Gain in Availability Regressed*	Availability Post-Survey
Administrative Leadership	School Staff	.58	.39	.26**
Personal Use of Innovations	School Staff	.34	.48	.41
Socio-Economic Status of Board Members	Board Members	.34	.33	—
Community Acceptance of Innovations	Board Members	.21	.23	.29
Knowledge about the Kettering-Colgate Project	Board Members	.20	.22	—
Diffusion to Groups	Innovating Teacher	—	—	.20
Financial Resources	Board Members	—	.10	.30
Multiple Correlation Coefficient		.72	.85	.89

TABLE XIII-3. Important School and Community Forces Influencing Differences in Usage of Innovations among the Experimental Group of Schools.

Variable (or Force)	As Perceived by	Gain in Usage	Gain in Usage Regressed*	Usage Post-Survey
Influence of the Kettering-Colgate Project	School Staff	.63	.24	.18**
Administrative Leadership	School Staff	.45	.30	.35
Personal Use of Innovations	School Staff	.25	.34	.38
Attitude Toward Modernization	Parents	.14	.29	.27
Maturity of Board (Years of Service)	Board Members	.04	.05	.03

(TABLE XIII-3. continued)

Variable (or Force)	As Perceived by	Gain in Attitude	Gain in Usage Regressed*	Usage Post-Survey
Diffusion among Individuals	School Staff	–	–	.05
Community Acceptance of Innovations	Board Members	–	.05	–
Multiple Correlation Coefficient		.65	.67	.70

Schools differ widely in innovative facilities.

*For a discussion of regressed gain, see Appendix B.
**Beta coefficients showing relative importance of each variable.
   Multiple correlation coefficients in bottom row are based on the variables for which Beta coefficients are shown.

CHAPTER 13
IMPLICATIONS

Critical problems face those who support constructive educational change. Action and resistance are doing daily battle in schools and colleges. Struggles occur in an orderly manner among school professionals, students and parents, and are kept in the family. More goes on than can or need be reported in the media. Only confrontations make the headlines. This study has implications for helping identify and resolve some of these problems.

Educational Lag

Identification of Problem. There has been no accurate way of estimating how far educational practice lags behind "know how". Some earlier writers placed the gap at fifty years. Lag exists in all fields. It is probably greater for service than in manufacturing endeavors because people may be harder to change than machines. In the present study one estimate of the magnitude of the lag can be made from the gap between the readiness (attitude) of the school professionals to innovate and the actual usage of innovation in the schools. School professionals were far above the neutral point in attitude (7 standard score units) but their schools were below the neutral point in usage (minus 1 standard score units). The size of the gap could be defined as 8 units. How many years would it take to overcome this lag? During the one-year action phase of the Kettering-Colgate Project, the schools gained approximately one standard unit. To make up 8 units would take 8 years. Even then the schools would not be modernized. They would be in the zone defined on the rating scale as using a moderate amount of innovation. It would take four more years to enter the zone defined on the scale as "a great deal" of usage. A total of fourteen years would be a conservative estimate of the time needed to bring the schools up to the level of usage that school professionals, and perhaps parents, desire now. School board members and parents were also above the neutral point in attitude toward modernization (by 4 to 5 standard score units). The problem is, how to close the gap and overcome the educational lag between attitude and practice.

Operational Plan. If schools were to harness the internal forces identified in the study, they would develop a plan that incorporated our findings related to administrative leadership, diffusion, health of the system, peer support and others. Evidence indicates that, given the training and opportunity, interested teachers will not only innovate, but will spread the word to board members, parents and others. This will be done voluntarily. The study has shown that the "ripple effect" is real in that other teachers can identify the department from which the "ripple" is coming. There is little doubt that the "ripple approach" will work in proportion to the amount of diffusion. This does not mean that the "ripple approach" is the best or only operational plan. If the evidence presented by the Innovating Teachers can be generalized, the implications are that some combination of the "ripple" and "restructuring" approach would be most effective.

Using this idea, schools would arrange a plan for training, encouraging and rewarding individual teachers who want to be creative. They could, at the same time, make long-range plans for restructuring. The "ripple approach" should remain as a continuing operation to provide diversity within the school. There is reason to believe that there may be advantages to having within the same school, teachers using different practices to take full advantage of teacher strengths and to provide diversity for students. A major implication brought out by the Innovating Teachers' reports is that the "ripple approach" must receive administrative and peer support. Therefore, the administration needs to provide some kind of an "umbrella" under which teachers can try new ideas without fear and with support.

School Forces. To have a quality school system, a school district must exert pressure for an administration that actively supports educational change and which is respected by the faculty for its competence and not for its legal authority alone. The administration must take the lead in developing a school climate of openness and trust, inquiry and creativeness that is essential to effective change. Neither the laissez-faire or the authoritarian type of administrator seems to produce an innovative climate. Schools whose faculty members are more knowledgeable about innovations and use them, seem not only to be more favorable toward innovations, but seem to gain more in favorability of response to outside efforts such as the Kettering-Colgate Project. In schools where many faculty members resist change, the "ripple" or some comparable approach would be a first step. More advanced schools might well direct their efforts at promoting an innovative climate, as described. In this study, the major internal force that influenced Usage and Availability, was administrative leadership. School-originated information about innovation seemed to have little influence on the faculty. Neither did the Kettering-Colgate Project brochure. What did have influence, was the Kettering-Colgate Project itself. It appears that schools should create some external cooperative organization, such as the Project or the Alliance, which would reinforce their creative efforts.

Discontinuity

Identification of Discontinuity Problem. Creative innovation is difficult to achieve without continuity. It cannot be turned on and off at the will of bureaus or legislators. The kinds of continuous support needed are educational and financial. State and federal support tends to come in one-year portions because of the financial connection with legislatures. Educational support, likewise, tends to be fickle because guidelines change, depending on who is in power. Leadership of governmental agencies in recent years has changed more often than the national presidency. Educational industries have learned that just as they get tooled to meet the demands for new materials and programs, the rug is pulled from under them.

Organizational Structure. To obtain continuity, the present study recommends that a program for innovations become an integral part of the legal organization structure of a region; that it be a cooperative endeavor of existing educational institutions; and that such a structure adopt the policy of educationally and financially supporting the program so that it would not be an undue hardship on any one local institution.

Student Participation

Identification of Problem. Students are more mature physically and mentally than they used to be. In recognition of this and for other reasons, eighteen-year olds have been given the right to vote. Student unrest has given schools and colleges an unfavorable image among those not close to the situation. In fact, students may be strong allies of constructive change. They are the consumers who can provide new ideas as to how they can best learn, but like consumers in the economic market, their pleas may be regarded with suspicion. Many people do not listen.

Effects on Students. The effect on students of a favorable faculty attitude toward

69

change seemed to be toward a greater awareness of their goals and a reduction in friction with fellow students. This study reveals that students were well aware that an innovative project was in progress and may have had some influence on the availability of innovations throughout the school. As the role of students changes toward greater responsibility, research may need to shift its emphasis from studying the effects of innovations on students to the affect of students on change.

Community Participation

Identification of Problem. There is a tendency not to consider parents as very powerful due to the fact that their influence is indirect. Other reasons may be the amount of time it would take for planning with them, the tendency to consider that laymen should not interfere with professional matters, and the fear of encouraging parents to be paternalistic with their children.

Community Forces. Parents, we have seen, have more indirect influence than is commonly believed. They have this because school board members base policy decisions, not on their own attitudes toward innovation, but on what they perceive the community attitude to be. It is suggested, therefore, that parents be kept well informed of new practices in the school. One effective way of doing this, verified in this study, was through brochures from an external source such as the Kettering-Colgate Project. School-originated information to the community did not seem to be effective, but this may have been because few had the time to prepare effective materials of this kind.

School board members did not seem to affect faculty Attitude, but they, like parents, did influence actual Availability and Usage of innovations. They exert important forces for facilitating or impeding constructive change. This study suggests that the most effective way to influence that board is through the parents. Obviously, the administrator has a strong influence on the Board.

Financial Resources. A major force influencing creative change is the financial resources, as perceived by parents and board members. New practices are the first to be cut in a financial squeeze. One way to impede change would be to emphasize the lack of funds. It is not necessarily the actual inadequacy of financial resources that impede change, but the parental and school board perception of that inadequacy for innovative purposes. It is suggested, that keeping the school up-to-date is a matter of priorities and that innovative climate, faculty attitude, parent enthusiasm, are not purchasable.

University Participation

Identification of the Problem. The society today calls on universities not only to teach, but to help with many of its large economic, social, scientific and educational problems. Independent universities draw most of their support from student tuition and cannot justify use of this source of funds to support even worthwhile social purposes, other than teaching. Those looking to the universities for leadership and inspiration are just beginning to realize that universities do not have unlimited resources. University research and leadership projects must have a clear relationship to the teaching of students or they will not be continued. A few universities, such as Johns Hopkins University, have discontinued their programs for teacher preparation. Others, such as Princeton University, have added the program within the last four years, but only because it was an important part of the education of students. Can universities afford to continue to serve the leadership and service role discussed in Part 1, and especially at the end of Chapter 2?

Implications for the University. A university finds that close cooperation with the schools in a project of this kind has a number of cross-benefits. It discovers that facilities for innovation in schools are of interest and benefit to its students, not only to those planning to teach, but to others. The proportion of undergraduates interested in educational change is high.

Working in an Alliance Project with the schools will improve the university's program for preparing teachers. It will help maintain a creative faculty and help the faculty to keep abreast of new practices in the schools so that they will be able to articulate the university program with that of the schools. Also, teaching interns (graduate students) can help reduce teachers' loads while they are innovating, and undergraduates serving as teacher aides or in other capacities can benefit both the schools and their own education.

Accountability

Identification of Problem. Lack of accountability means paucity of research and evaluation for new practices being attempted in local schools. Observation suggests that budget items for improvement of instruction and innovation are cut first. Traditional or habitual practices seem more immune. If boards of education had evidence that new practices were indeed improvements in accomplishing the schools' objectives, priorities might be reversed. Feedback, at present, is for the most part hearsay.

Research Evaluation. The present study was inaugurated with the intent of preparing an organized set of instruments, research designs and other tools for monitoring important forces. These are discussed throughout the report and especially in Appendices B and D. Much remains to be done but can be accomplished through cooperative efforts.

APPENDICES

APPENDIX A

GAINS IN INNOVATIVE ATTITUDES, AVAILABILITY AND USAGE
FOR THE KETTERING PROJECT SCHOOLS (1968 – 1970) (DESIGN II)

Attitude Gain

A ten-item attitude scale was administered to all school personnel in 1968 (Pre-test) and again in 1970 (Post-test) to the same individuals. Results were available for twenty-six experimental schools and eleven control schools. Table A-1 shows that the experimental schools as a group made a significant gain in attitude from where they were at pre-test time, 1968. (Actual t = 2.3; Needed t = 1.7) Most of this gain was due to five of the experimental schools (14, 17, 22, 25 and 26), each of which made a significant attitude gain. None of the others had a significant loss. Finding that some experimental schools did show a significant gain is important because a study could then be made of forces related to that gain with some hope of finding relationships.

On the other hand, three of the control schools (61, 63, and 71) made a significant gain and none showed a significant loss. One would conclude therefore that there was no difference in the proportion of gains in attitude toward innovation between the experimental and control group of schools. Of interest is the finding, shown in Column 8 of Table A-1, that nineteen of the experimental school faculties were significantly favorable toward innovation at the end of the experiment (above the neutral point of 3.8). A large majority of both the control and experimental schools were significantly above the neutral point in faculty attitude toward innovation at the close of the experiment.

Availability Gain

Table A-2 provides information with respect to availability of innovations in each school. Twelve of the twenty-six schools made a significant gain in availability. None showed a significant loss. On the average, a difference in Columns 3 and 6 of 4.0 is needed to indicate significance beyond chance.

As a group the 26 experimental schools gained an average of 3 points in availability beyond what the comparison school gained (1 point). This gain is significant at the .05 level (t = 2.2).

Of interest is the comparison of the level of each of the schools to the neutral point 33. (Which means that a "moderate" amount of innovation was available.) At the beginning of the experiment seven (7) of the experimental schools were above this norm: nineteen were below. Two years later, fifteen were above that point, and eleven were below. Nine of the schools which were below before the experiment were above at the end. (Chi Square = 6.4, Needed 3.8 at .05 level).

Usage Gain

Table A-2 Columns 4 and 7, show that nineteen of the experimental schools made a significant gain in usage. None showed a significant loss. Seven of the experimental schools made a gain in usage significantly beyond that made by the comparison school (1.75 points). Five made a significantly less gain than it did. On the average, the 26 experimental schools gained one point more than the comparison school but this was not enough to be significant at the .05 level.

TABLE A-1. Change in Faculty Attitude Toward Innovations Among the Experimental and Control Schools.

EXPERIMENTAL

School	N	Mean (Pre)	Mean (Post)	Gain	t (gain)	r pre-vs. post	Past-Attitude vs. Neutral Point
1	22	3.25	3.54	-.29	-0.89	.38	.78
2	24	3.36	3.86	-.50	-1.78	.71	.16
3	36	2.98	2.75	.23	1.42	.51	5.74*
4	21	2.66	2.50	.15	1.62	.93	5.61*
5	31	2.91	3.40	-.49	-1.84	.35	1.43
6	16	3.19	3.27	-.08	-0.31	.51	1.86
7	25	2.88	2.78	.10	.58	.57	5.05*
9	24	2.95	2.82	.12	.62	.22	5.28*
10	36	2.79	2.60	-.19	1.23	-.11	8.85*
11	12	2.78	3.30	-.52	-1.17	.74	1.02
12	18	2.66	2.73	-.07	-0.24	.33	3.35*
13	5	3.30	3.06	.24	.80	.87	1.41
14	26	2.70	2.38	.32	4.65*	.29	27.01*
15	29	2.87	2.63	.23	1.36	.21	7.08*
16	25	3.01	2.93	.08	.33	.46	3.66*
17	14	3.09	2.61	.48	3.12*	.21	8.91*
18	26	3.06	3.04	.02	.13	.69	3.44*
19	49	2.90	3.15	-.25	-1.56	.63	2.96*
20	20	2.71	2.61	.10	.49	.56	4.81*
21	23	2.90	2.76	.14	.50	-.14	4.62*
22	9	2.66	2.41	.24	3.19*	.53	41.70*
23	84	2.93	2.96	-.04	-0.32	.27	7.13*
24	17	2.82	2.57	.25	1.44	.35	6.95*
25	39	3.00	2.64	.36	2.75*	.29	9.79*
26	27	2.86	2.55	.31	2.13*	.60	7.99*

CONTROL

School	N	Mean (Pre)	Mean (Post)	Gain	t (gain)	r	Post vs. Neutral Point
61	17	3.05	2.62	.44	2.88*	.18	9.81*
62	23	2.74	2.73	.02	.08	.66	3.54*
63	31	2.91	2.55	.37	3.41*	.42	11.89*
64	17	2.94	2.62	.31	1.19	.45	4.16*
65	9	2.87	2.77	.10	.21	-.04	2.67*
66	23	2.81	2.69	.12	.64	.37	5.60*
67	37	2.66	2.68	-.01	-0.10	.59	6.50*
68	16	3.19	3.06	.14	.47	.38	2.50*
70	12	3.22	3.76	-.54	-1.62	.75	.11
71	38	3.04	2.62	.42	2.55*	.30	8.34*
72	21	3.03	2.77	.26	1.10	.39	4.41*

*t tests: (1) For individual schools (at .05 level, needed t = 1.98) (2) For overall gain of 26 schools, t = 2.3 (at .05 level, needed t = 2.06).

Also, in columns 2 and 3, a low score means a more favorable attitude.

TABLE A-2. Level of Usage and Availability and Gains, of Innovations in the Experimental Schools (N = 27)

School	Usage			Availability		
	Pre	Post	Gain	Pre	Post	Gain
1	36.3	33.8	- 2.5	38.3	35.2	- 2.5
2	24.5	41.3	16.8*	24.5	40.2	15.7*
3	37.7	37.0	- 0.7	40.6	37.2	- 3.4
4	29.3	31.5	2.2	30.3	30.0	- 0.3
5	30.0	42.8	12.8*	29.6	40.5	10.8*
6	29.0	30.8	1.8	29.6	29.2	- 0.4
7	28.5	32.0	3.5	28.5	26.7	- 1.7
8	43.3	37.3	- 6.0	49.3	42.2	- 7.1*
9	37.5	42.8	5.3	39.2	38.2	- 1.0
10	30.5	30.5	0.0	30.0	31.0	1.0
11	26.0	31.5	5.5	29.3	26.7	- 2.5
12	24.0	38.8	14.8*	24.0	33.2	9.2*
13	30.0	30.5	0.5	30.6	26.7	- 3.9
14	38.3	36.5	- 1.8	35.3	38.2	2.9
15	29.0	39.8	10.8*	33.7	45.0	11.2*
16	30.3	29.0	- 1.3	29.3	39.2	9.9*
17	25.0	31.5	6.5*	26.5	31.5	5.0
18	34.0	32.0	- 2.0	32.0	39.0	7.0*
19	38.8	42.0	3.2	39.7	37.2	- 2.5
20	27.5	29.8	2.3	24.5	34.5	10.0*
21	27.0	38.8	11.8*	30.0	34.5	4.5
22	27.7	32.0	4.3	26.3	31.5	5.1
23	27.5	34.0	6.5*	26.5	35.0	8.5*
24	23.0	30.8	7.8	23.3	25.2	1.9
25	44.0	33.3	-10.7*	44.0	30.0	-14.0*
26	25.7	33.3	7.6	28.0	32.0	4.0
27	32.3	37.5	5.2	32.3	37.7	5.4
All Schools	31.0	34.3	3.3	31.7	34.4	2.7

NOTE: t test of significance of gains: (1) Usage gain, t = 2.17 (2) Availability gain, t = 2.16**
*Significance at the .05 level.

Conclusions

1. The experimental group made a significant gain in attitude (at the .05 level). However, the proportion of experimental schools gaining was not sufficiently different than the proportion for the control schools gaining. Five out of twenty-five experimental schools and three control schools out of eleven, gained significantly.

2. Compared to their initial status, the experimental schools as a group showed a significant gain in both availability and usage over the two-year period. However, when contrasted to the "comparison school" they, as a group, made a significant gain in availability but not in usage.

3. Within the experimental group of twenty-six schools, rather large changes in availability and usage occurred. The ranges were −11.0 to +18.8, and −10.7 to

+16.8 respectively. Thus, the data showed promise for further analysis of forces in the schools and community that might be related to these gains. (See Chapters 6 to 13.)

Usage was defined as the extent to which curricular, technological and structural innovations were used throughout the school.

THE NATURE OF THE INSTRUMENTS AND THEIR
RELIABILITY AND VALIDITY

There is a growing interest by school systems in research and evaluation instruments. Education is being called upon more and more to justify its expenditures and to demonstrate that changes are effective. It is urgent that evaluators carefully choose both instruments and research designs. One of the purposes of this project has been to develop improved research instruments for measuring change and variables related to it. Of major importance in this respect has been the development of those that accurately measure school and community forces.

Appendix B will first concern itself with the criteria. It will describe the instruments, present evidence about the reliability and validity and then comment as to their usefulness, accuracy, and provide the sample instrument. It will then proceed to a similar presentation of instruments measuring school and community forces and other variables.

Determination of instrument reliability has been approached indirectly through a study of the stability of responses of the same individuals over a two-year period. Correlation coefficients between pre- and post-tests, as indices of this stability, were made up of two influences: (1) the extent of real change in standings among the schools; and (2) the extent to which the instruments were reliable. If, for example, the pre- vs. post-correlation was .6, we knew that the reliability coefficient was no lower than .6. In fact, it was probably higher because of the interventions that have occurred during the two-year span. A more direct procedure for determining reliability would have been to re-administer the same instruments a few days apart. This would have been difficult, if not impossible. Parents, board members and teachers are busy people.

Evidence on the validity of the criteria and other measures will be presented by correlating measures obtained from two different sources, such as from outside raters and from teachers, or parents, or board members. Examples of instruments will be included so that others may use them.

Reliability and Validity of the Criteria
Attitude Toward Innovation Scale (ATI)

Description. This ten-item scale was developed by the project staff members. Two equivalent forms can be prepared from the thirty-five items listed. These are statements that are commonly made about innovations, and range from very favorable to unfavorable.

Subjects. The items were judged to be favorable or unfavorable by three groups, totaling 83 students. The scale was constructed, using the Thurstone-Likert technique described in the article above and available from the author. In this study it was administered to all professional personnel in the experimental and control schools in the pre- and post-survey.

Response Mode. Subjects place a check mark beside those items with which they agree.

Scoring. The person's score is the median scale value of the items endorsed by him as "agree". Low scores indicate a favorable attitude toward innovations. Other scales of this type produce test re-rest reliability coefficients of .70 to .85 when the lapsed time interval is short. A safe estimate of the reliability coefficient, based on the pre-post survey figure, would be .80.

Reliability. Table B-1 shows the correlation coefficients between pre- and post-survey times for three of the major criteria. It indicates that faculty attitude toward innovations, as measured by the ten-item ATI test, was quite stable among the schools in the two-year period (r = .66). We can be quite sure that the reliability coefficient is no lower than .66.

Validity. The validity of the scale is based on correlations of .55 to .65 with five item multiple-choice set of questions on the IEP survey (pre- and post-) (See Table B-2). The scores of professional persons in each school were summed to obtain a score for that school for the two instruments. Correlation coefficients (.55 and .65) show the relative standings of the schools at the time of each survey.

Comments. This is a satisfactorily valid and reliable scale for measuring attitude toward innovations in a school. It was limited to 10 items to save time and space during the survey. In reducing the scale from the normal 17 items to 10, the most unfavorable items were omitted. This was done because preliminary observations indicated that the population was slightly favorable. The most unfavorable items, thus, would not be checked by the respondees: many unused items would be printed. If a research study needs the longer scale, including the most negative items, seventeen items or more may be selected from the list given in Exhibit B-1.

TABLE B-1. Correlation Coefficients Showing Stability (or Change) on Criterion Measures Among Experimental Schools (N = 26) Over the Two-Year Period.

		Correlation Coefficient
Faculty Attitude Toward Innovation	(Pre vs. Post)	.66
Availability of Innovations	(Pre vs. Post)	.27
Actual Usage of Innovations	(Pre vs. Post)	.25

TABLE B-2. Validity Coefficients for the Attitude Toward Innovations Scale; (1) the Ten-item Thurstone-Likert Type Scale (AS 1) vs. (2) Multiple Choice Scale (IEP – 5 items)

		Thurstone-Likert vs. Multiple Choice Validity Coefficient	
		(Pearson's r)	Regressed
1. Pre-Survey (Attitude)	1 vs. 2	.55	.55
2. Post-Survey (Attitude)	1 vs. 2	.65	.65
3. Gain (Attitude)	1 vs. 2	.28	.46

EXHIBIT B-1. Attitude Toward Innovations Scale (ATI)

Directions: The statements that follow relate to beliefs that you may have about curricular and technological innovations such as those mentioned in this booklet. "Place a checkmark (✓) beside each statement with which you agree."

Order Low-High	Item	Scale Value	Flanagan's r
1.	These innovations have more demerit than merit . . .	7.00	.69
2.	*These innovations do not impress me favorably.	6.98	.90
3.	*Educators probably don't have the proof to support their claims for most of these innovations . . .	6.63	.46
4.	*Most innovations that are tried are not very bad, but they are not very good either . . .	5.47	.73
5.	*The school would be neither better nor worse off with these innovations . . .	5.04	.47
6.	The innovations are probably effective but I am really not sure . . .	4.56	.53
7.	Such innovations may not be much more expensive than current practices in the same classroom . . .	3.82	.71
8.	I feel that it would be better if the school system adopted these innovations than if it rejected them . . .	3.21	.79
9.	*Under an innovative school program classroom learning will become more efficient . . .	2.89	.74
10.	*I welcome the adoptions of such innovations by the school system . . .	2.61	.73
11.	*The introduction of innovations in local schools may result in more demand for highly qualified teachers . . .	2.47	—
12.	Most of these innovations suggest wonderful possibilities for our schools . . .	2.31	.83
13.	*These innovations can be depended upon to improve student learning . . .	2.27	.61
14.	*These innovations will solve some of the school's greatest problems . . .	1.70	.64
15.	*An attempt to innovate represents one of the most dynamic advances a school system can make . . .	1.35	.72
16.	The school would be better off without this type of innovation . . .	7.61	.74
17.	I do not believe the recent innovations in instruction adopted by the system have aided the pupils . . .	6.98	.65
18.	The school would get along just as well without the innovations . . .	6.63	.70
19.	The successful use of these innovations may result in higher taxes . . .	6.45	.65
20.	I am really not sure whether these innovations have aided the pupils . . .	5.28	.53

Order Low-High	Item	Scale Value	Flanagan's r
21.	The innovations are not bad but they are not good either.	5.18	.73
22.	I am not against the use of the innovations . . .	4.08	.53
23.	Such innovations may not be much more expensive than current practices in the same classrooms . . .	3.82	.71
24.	I feel that it would be better if the school system adopted these innovations than if it rejected them . . .	3.21	.79
25.	These types of innovations have more merit than demerit . . .	2.88	.70
26.	The adoption of these innovations would have a positive effect on increasing the teachers' ability to instruct their pupils . . .	2.34	.82
27.	The students are sure to be benefited by these innovations . . .	1.75	.74
28.	The innovations bring the level of instruction of our pupils to a new peak.	1.50	.57
29.	A good many of the innovations proposed for schools are absurd . . .	8.94	—
30.	The introduction of new technological devices into the schools is about the most worthless kind of innovation . . .	8.92	—
31.	Many innovations turn out to be a waste of time . . .	8.25	—
32.	Teachers in our schools should not adopt untried methods at the expense of tried methods . . .	7.98	—
33.	This trend of introducing innovations will increase until it gets out of hand . . .	7.75	—
34.	Many innovations waste money that could be better used for other purposes . . .	7.61	—
35.	Most innovations actually decrease student interest in a subject . . .	7.22	—

The 10 items used in the post-survey. The other five items were in the pre-survey. Five items were common to both. Items 16 to 35 were not used.

Hamilton Innovative Profile (HIP — Availability and Usage)

Descriptions. This eighty-five item rating profile was developed by the project staff in 1968 to measure the level to which a school had developed with respect to availability and usage of innovations. The items covered curricular, technological, and instructional innovations, and their organizational effectiveness.

Response Made by Raters. Raters interviewed two to four key professionals in each of the 26 schools, including an administrator and counselor. They toured the building, observing eight listed features. They then recorded their ratings on a scale (see Exhibit B-2) for each item to indicate the standing of the school on that item.

Scoring. Not all items were used in the scoring. Eleven of the items were selected on the basis of a standard step-wise regression procedure. The scale is from 0 to 100 ("Not at all" to "A great deal"). A school at the middle point on the scale, meaning a "moderate amount" would receive a score of 33. The scale was constructed so as to have sufficient room at the top for schools to show gain.

Reliability and Validity. Table B-1 shows that the correlation coefficients between pre- and post-survey ratings for availability and usage were .27 and .25, respectively. Not much can be inferred about reliability from these. However, the validity coefficients shown in Table B-3, show correlations between usage as measured by the outside raters and usage, as reported by the teachers on the pre-survey instrument (IEP) to be .55. The minimum reliability coefficient needed to produce a .55 correlation is over .74 on each measure. This is reasonably high considering that the raters were viewing the total school program while teachers were responding to eight specific innovations.

Comments

This availability and usage scale seems to have moderate validity and reliability for research uses. Its use is time-consuming. Raters can visit an average of only two schools a day.

Further study is needed to develop an instrument that will be less time-consuming. That this is possible, is suggested by the validity coefficient of .55, reported above. One such inventory of 25 items was developed but not used because of the potential of overloading the professional staff of the schools with paper work. To construct such an instrument, several obvious research problems need to be settled, such as (1) which types of school staff give most valid ratings; and (2) can they be provided a common reference point, so that differences among schools will reflect the true situation.

TABLE B-3. Validity Coefficients of the Usage Scale of Innovations (Raters' Judgments, HIP) Compared to Teacher's Judgments (IEP) (N = 21 schools)

		Raters' vs. Teachers' Judgments	
		(Pearson's r)	Regressed
1.	Pre-Survey Usage	.55	.55
2.	Post-Survey Usage	.48	.40
3.	Gain in Usage	.42	.38

Exhibit B-2 – Hamilton Innovation Profile*

Instructions to Raters

You are to interview two qualified informants and subsequently make estimates about the amount of usage of educational media and curricula materials. You should base these estimates on your observations and on your familiarity with the reference school.

The first person to interview should be the most knowledgeable administrator; the second should be the most knowledgeable guidance person available. As a rule, interview no one with less than two years' experience obtained in that building. Conduct your interview in the building in a room most advantageous to observation whenever possible. Interview the informant when he is alone. Each rater should take turns asking questions. The statements on the interview schedule have logical divisions that should facilitate such a procedure.

Do not discuss this questionnaire with the informant. You may state that you are verifying the accuracy of the past year's research. In addition, each one of you serves as a check on the other.

If you cannot arrange an appointment with both persons, report this to the office. If an interview will interfere with lunch or supper, invite the informant to be your guest. Promptly submit an expense voucher to the office.

Scale

(A) ———— (B) ———— (C) ———— (D) ———— (E)

81

---

*The eleven items summed to obtain the criteria scores.

Usage
(Prior to May 1, 1970)

To what extent (during the past two years) . . .

26. has the school used the space for storage of instructional media and new curricular materials?

27. has the staff used the instructional materials resource center?

28. *has the staff used these production facilities for producing materials other than dittoes and stencils?

29. has the staff used the services of an audio-visual coordinator?

30. *did the audio-visual coordinator provide consultant services about new instructional media?

31. has the curriculum coordinator provided consultant services about new curricular materials?

32. did paraprofessionals assist in the production (and preparation of) instructional materials?

33. has the school obtained funds for new instructional media and curricular materials?

34. has the school used its budget allocation for new instructional media and curricular materials?

35. did the school produce materials about new instructional media and curricular materials?

Availability
(Since May 1, 1968)

To what extent (during the past two years) . . .

1. . . . Is there space available for storage of instructional media and new curricular materials?

2. . . . does the school have an instructional materials resource center?

3. . . . are production facilities available to the staff for producing materials other than dittoes and stencils?

4. . . . does the staff have access to the services of an audio-visual coordinator?

5. . . . is the audio-visual coordinator capable of providing consultant services about new instructional media?

6. . . . is the curriculum coordinator capable of providing consultant services about new curricular materials?

7. . . . does the school employ paraprofessionals?

8. . . . has the school applied to outside agencies for funds for new instructional media and curricular materials?

9. . . . did the school's budget for the past two years contain an allocation for new instructional media and curricular materials?

10. . . . does the school circulate materials about new instructional media and curricular materials?

*The Eleven Items Used For The Availability and Usage Scale.

Availability
(Since May 1, 1968)

11.*. . . does the school's professional library contain books especially pertinent to innovation?

12.*. . . does the school subscribe to periodicals especially pertinent to innovation?

13. . . . do staff have access to instructional space that permits large and small group instruction?

14.*. . . do staff have access to a room suitable for multi-media presentations?

15. . . . does the school provide wet carrells for independent study?

16. . . . has the staff encouraged students to make presentations using new instructional media and curricular materials?

17. . . . has the staff seriously considered moving toward a system of flexible scheduling?

18. . . . has the staff seriously considered moving toward a form of team teaching?

19. . . . has the mathematics department planned to use new concepts in mathematics instruction?

20. . . . has the science department planned to use new concepts in science instruction?

21.*. . . has the English department planned to use new concepts in English instruction?

*The Eleven Items Used For The Availability and Usage Scale.

Usage
(Prior to May 1, 1970)

36.*did the staff read books especially pertinent to innovation (Trump, Miles, Allen, etc.)?

37.*did the staff read these periodicals especially pertinent to innovation (A-V Instruction, etc.)?

38. did the staff vary the size of their instructional space to accommodate large and small group instructions?

39.*did the staff use a room for multi-media presentations?

40. did students use wet carrells for independent study?

41. have students made presentations using new instructional media and curricular materials?

42. has the school's organization moved toward a system of flexible scheduling?

43. has the staff organization moved toward a form of team teaching?

44. has the mathematics department made use of new concepts in mathematics instruction?

45. has the science department made use of new concepts in science instruction?

46.*has the English department made use of new concepts in English instruction?

Availability
(Since May 1, 1968)

Usage
(Prior to May 1, 1970)

22. . . has the social studies department planned to use new concepts in social studies instruction?

23. . . have other departments planned to use new concepts of instruction in their fields?

24. . . does the staff continually monitor the effectiveness of new instructional media and curricular materials?

25. In terms of observed extent of availability of instructional support how does this school compare with the reference school?

   A. Much Below
   B. Below
   C. Same
   D. Above
   E. Much Above

Card 1

Card 2

47. has the social studies department made use of new concepts in social studies instruction?

48. have other departments made use of new concepts of instruction in their fields?

49. has the staff monitored the effectiveness of new instructional media and curricular materials?

50. In terms of observed extent of usage how does this school compare with the reference school?

   A. Much Below
   B. Below
   C. Same
   D. Above
   E. Much Above

51. . . does the school encourage teachers to use new media and curricular materials?

76. has the staff used new instructional media and curricular materials?

Availability
(Since May 1, 1968)

52. ... may the staff place orders for new media and curricular materials?

53. *... did you expect the use of new media and curricular materials to increase during the last two years?

54. *... does the school encourage its staff to share their experiences with new instructional media and curricular materials?

55. *... has the school encouraged (e.g. with funds, etc.) attendance at specialized conferences and workshops on new instructional media and curricular materials?

56. *... does the staff try to coordinate its various curricula toward the attainment of general, school-wide objectives?

57. ... does the staff try to integrate new instructional media within curricula?

58. *... does the school favor some provision for individual rates of progress (individualizing instruction)?

59. ... do plans for renovation and expansion next year include provisions for new instructional media and curricular materials?

60. ... do you feel that this instrument is accurate?

Usage
(Prior to May 1, 1970)

77. has the staff requested the school to study new instructional media and curricular materials?

78. did the use of new instructional media and curricular materials increase during the past two years?

79. *have the staff shared their experiences with new instructional media and curricular materials?

80. have staff members during the past two years attended specialized conferences and workshops on new instructional media and curricular materials?

81. *has the staff coordinated its various curricula toward the attainment of general, school-wide objectives?

82. has the schcol integrated new instructional media within curricula?

83. *has the school made provision for individual rates of progress (individualizing instruction)?

84. did plans for renovation and expansion during the past two years include provisions for new instructional media and curricular materials?

85. do you feel that the informant's responses to your questions are accurate?

OBSERVATION CHART

Use this list as a guide on your inspection tour prior to beginning the interview.

1. Storage space for instructional materials
2. Instructional materials resource center
3. Production facilities
4. Professional library
5. Large-small group instructional areas
6. Multimedia presentation area
7. Wet Carrells
8. Teacher aides

Instruments for Measuring Community and School Forces
The Survey Instrument for Board Members and Parents (BOPAR)

Description. This fifteen-item inventory was developed by the staff of the project. The pre-survey instrument included demographic items. Its last nine items were questions about activities and attitudes and were the same for parents and board members. The post-survey instrument eliminated the demographic items because these were now determined. It added items about the influence of the Kettering Project and brochures and concerning new influences that might have affected change.

Subjects. The items were administered without further refinement to all 154 school board members and a random sampling of parents (867) in the twenty-six school districts.

Response Made. Subjects underlined one of five spaces on an answer card to indicate their responses, and returned the card in a sealed, self-addressed envelope.

Scoring. Each item was considered a separate variable and was coded from 1 to 5 for data processing.

Stability and Reliability. Five items in the BOPAR were identical on the pre- and post-survey instruments. Table B-4 shows the correlation coefficients between the responses of the same individuals in 1968 and 1970. All but one of these correlations is significant at the .05 level of probability. From these data, one could conclude, for example, that the five-choice item, "Which phrase best describes your community's rate of acceptance of innovations at the secondary school level?" has a reliability coefficient of at least .49 for board members. The reliability coefficient is probably higher than this for reasons previously discussed. This is substantiated by the fact that the correlation between two similar items on the pre-test measuring variable I (for board members) is .65, compared to the .21 shown in Table B-4. For parents, the same two items correlated .43 on the pre-test. On the post-test two similar and contiguous items (Items III-1 and III-2) produced a correlation coefficient of .73 for teachers (N = 689).

TABLE B-4. Relationships between the Pre- and Post-Survey Characteristics and Attitudes of the Board Members and of Parents in the Twenty-six Experimental Schools. (N = 131 and 867, respectively.)

Variable	Board Members r (pre- vs. post-)* N = 131	Parents r (pre- vs. post-)* N = 867
1. Attitude toward Innovations (item 10 pre- vs 13 post)	.21	.36
2. Attitude toward Innovations (item 11 pre- vs 14 post)	.43	.22
3. Attitude toward Modernization	.20	.22
4. Community Attitude toward Innovation	.49	.24
5. Community Desire for a Quality Program	.49	.35

*A Pearson's r of .19 is needed for significance at the .05 level.

Comments

Most of the items on this inventory are sufficiently reliable for exploratory research purposes. They need to be refined and tested further for their adequacy for assessing community forces related to change. They offer promising leads.

Exhibit B-3 – Board-Parent Inventory (BOPAR)

Definition: The term, secondary school, means the local public junior high or middle school, as well as senior high.

SAMPLE QUESTION

X.   How many miles do you live from the local secondary school?
   A.   Less than 1
   B.   1 – 3
   C.   4 – 6
   D.   7 – 10
   E.   More than 10

Select the one category that best describes the distance from your home to the school. Find the SAMPLE QUESTION box on your card. Darken with a soft pencil the letter of the category you selected.
For example:
SAMPLE QUESTION: X (A) (B) (C) (D) (E)   Answer card

For each question below mark on the card the one appropriate category for each question as you have done for the SAMPLE QUESTION.

Pre-Survey: Items used for Board Member Pre-Survey Only.

1.   How many years have you served on the school board?
   A.   Less than 2
   B.   2 – 5
   C.   6 – 9
   D.   10 – 12
   E.   More than 12
2.   What is your age in years approximately?
   A.   Under 21
   B.   21 – 35
   C.   36 – 50
   D.   51 – 65
   E.   Over 65
3.   How many children do you have in the local secondary school?
   A.   None
   B.   1
   C.   2
   D.   3
   E.   4 or more
4.   What is the highest level you have reached in school?
   A.   Less than a high school diploma
   B.   A high school diploma
   C.   More than a high school but less than a college diploma
   D.   A college diploma
   E.   More than a college diploma
5.   How would you describe your financial situation in relation to the approximate national family average ($6000 – $8000)?

A. Much less than average
B. Less than average
C. Average
D. More than average
E. Much more than average

6. Which one of these do you feel has the most influence in making decisions about new ideas and techniques in the local public high school?
   A. The supervising principal or superintendent
   B. The high school principal
   C. The secondary school faculty
   D. The school board
   E. A curriculum coordinator or department head

Pre-Survey: Items used for Parent Pre-Survey Only.

For each question below mark on the card the one appropriate category for each question as you have done for the SAMPLE QUESTION.

1. How many years have you lived in this school district?
   A. Less than 2
   B. 2 – 5
   C. 6 – 9
   D. 10 – 12
   E. More than 12

2. What is your age in years approximately?
   A. Under 21
   B. 21 – 35
   C. 36 – 50
   D. 51 – 65
   E. Over 65

3. How many children do you have in the secondary school?
   A. None
   B. 1
   C. 2
   D. 3
   E. 4 or more

4. What is the highest level you have reached in school?
   A. Less than a high school diploma
   B. A high school diploma
   C. More than a high school but less than a college diploma
   D. A college diploma
   E. More than a college diploma

5. How would you describe your financial situation in relation to the approximate national family average ($6000 – $8000)?
   A. Much less than average
   B. Less than average
   C. Average
   D. More than average
   E. Much more than average

6. How interested are you in the local secondary school?
   A. Not at all
   B. Somewhat

C. Moderately
D. Quite
E. Very

Pre-Survey: Items Common to both Board Members and Parents.

7. How often do you exercise your right to vote at annual school elections?
    A. Never
    B. Sometimes
    C. Often
    D. Very Often
    E. Always

8. How much information do you come in contact with about new ideas and techniques used at the local secondary school?
    A. Very little
    B. A little
    C. Some
    D. Considerable
    E. A great deal

9. Which phrase best describes your community's rate of acceptance of new ideas and techniques at the secondary school level?
    A. Very slow
    B. Rather slow
    C. About equally slow and rapid
    D. Rather rapid
    E. Very rapid

10. How much support would you give local efforts to raise money for new ideas and techniques in the secondary school?
    A. Very little
    B. A little
    C. Some
    D. Considerable
    E. A great deal

11. Which category best describes your own attitude toward the introduction of new ideas and techniques in the local secondary school?
    A. Very unfavorable
    B. Quite unfavorable
    C. About equally favorable and unfavorable
    D. Quite favorable
    E. Very favorable

12. How important to your community is it that the local secondary school be up-to-date in its ways of educating students?
    A. Not at all
    B. Somewhat
    C. Moderately
    D. Quite
    E. Very

13. In your estimation how concerned is your community about the quality of education in the local secondary school?
    A. Very little
    B. Little

C. Moderately
D. Quite
E. Very

14. How much confidence do you have that, given the means, the local secondary school faculty is capable of using new ideas and techniques?
    A. Very little
    B. A little
    C. Some
    D. Considerable
    E. A great deal

15. In your opinion, how much is the local community financially able to do for students in its secondary school?
    A. No more than at present
    B. Slightly more than at present
    C. Moderately more than at present
    D. Quite a bit more than at present
    E. A great deal more than at present

Post-Survey: Items for both Board Members and Parents.

1. How much do you know about innovation at the local secondary school?
   A. Very little
   B. Little
   C. Some
   D. Considerable
   E. A great deal

2. How much do you know about the innovation supported by the Kettering Project at your local secondary school?
   A. Very little
   B. Little
   C. Some
   D. Considerable
   E. A great deal

3. How important to your community is it that the local secondary school try new ways of educating students?
   A. Not at all
   B. Somewhat
   C. Moderately
   D. Quite
   E. Very

4. In your opinion, how responsive is the local secondary school to the community's attitude toward innovation?
   A. Not at all
   B. Somewhat
   C. Moderately
   D. Quite
   E. Very

5. In your opinion, how adequate are local financial resources for supporting innovations?
   A. Very inadequate
   B. Quite inadequate

91

C. About equally adequate and inadequate
D. Quite adequate
E. Very adequate

6. What kind of effect has the reduction of state aid had on community attitudes toward innovation?
A. Very negative
B. Quite negative
C. Neither positive or negative
D. Quite positive
E. Very positive

7. What kind of effect have teacher salary negotiations had on community attitudes toward innovation?
A. Very negative
B. Quite negative
C. About equally negative and positive
D. Quite positive
E. Very positive

8. Which phrase best describes your community's rate of acceptance of innovations at the secondary school level?
A. Very slow
B. Rather Slow
C. About equally slow and rapid
D. Rather rapid
E. Very rapid

9. In your estimation, how concerned is your community about the quality of education at the local secondary school?
A. Very little
B. Little
C. Some
D. Considerable
E. A great deal

10. In your opinion, how much pressure should parents in your community exert to have innovations introduced into the local secondary school?
A. Very little
B. Little
C. Some
D. Considerable
E. A great deal

11. In general, how satisfied are you with the education that your child is (children are) receiving at the local secondary school?
A. Not at all
B. Somewhat
C. Moderately
D. Quite
E. Very

12. How important to you is it that the administrators of the secondary school be persons who actively work to support change and innovation?
A. Not at all
B. Somewhat
C. Moderately

    D. Quite
    E. Very
13. How much support would you give local efforts to raise money for innovations at the local secondary school?
    A. Very little
    B. Little
    C. Some
    D. Considerable
    E. A great deal
14. Which category best describes your own attitude toward the introduction of new ideas and techniques at the local secondary school?
    A. Very unfavorable
    B. Quite unfavorable
    C. About equally favorable and unfavorable
    D. Quite favorable
    E. Very favorable

Note: If you have seen a copy of the Kettering brochure, *Taking Part in Secondary School Innovation,* please answer the following question. If you did not see a copy, please leave this question blank.

15. In your estimation, how much has seeing the brochure influenced your attitude toward innovation?
    A. Not at all
    B. Somewhat
    C. Moderately
    D. Quite
    E. Very

The Inventory of Educational Practices (IEP)

Description. This forty-item instrument was constructed by the project staff. For the pre-survey, it contained forty items and for the post-survey, thirty-seven items. (The ATI instrument was printed as part of the former and both the ATI and COPED were published as part of the latter.) The items gathered information of five types: (1) communication of information about innovation inside and outside of the school; (2) awareness of innovation through training and understanding of what was going on in the school; (3) personal usage of information; (4) attitude and involvement of self and others toward innovations; (5) who influenced the introduction of innovations; and (6) the influence of the Kettering Project and brochure. Seven items were nominal and the balance were ordinal scales.

Subjects: The instruments were administered to all the teachers, administrators and other personnel in the twenty-six schools.

Response Mode: Each person checks one of five answers to indicate his choice. Choices for the ordinal type items are usually from "a great deal" (scored 5) to "none" (scored 1), "very effective" to "very ineffective," or such appropriate phrases.

Scoring: For the most part each item was used as a separate variable in the testing of the hypothesis. There were occasions, however, when items were combined to form alternate criteria, to check the validity of the original six criteria. For example, items II-3 through 10 were combined to form what was called the Usage 2 criterion. Items IV-4 through 7 were combined to form the Attitude 2 criterion.

93

Reliability and Validity: Table B-5 shows the correlation coefficients of similar individual items on the post-survey instrument. They vary from .62 to .86 and average .78, and are considered to be approximations of the reliability of the items. The coefficients are among schools, and show extent to which personnel agree as to the relative standing of the schools on each of the paired items. For example, the response of all teachers in each school on item IV-4 — attitude toward rapidity of change, were averaged to obtain 26 averages. The same procedure was followed for item IV-7 — attitude toward innovations. The resulting correlation coefficient between the two variables for the 26 schools was .80.

Validity can best be discussed by reference to Table B-3. This table shows the extent of agreement as to the standing of the schools, obtained from data from two independent sources. It shows that the alternate eight-item criterion (based on teachers' estimates of school usage correlated .55 with outside experts' rating of school usage. For the post-tests, the extent of agreement was .48. Table B-1 shows that the ATI attitude scale correlated .55 with the alternate five-item criteria (IET) for the pre-survey, and .65 for the post-survey.

Comments. The items in this instrument seem to have sufficient reliability and validity to be used for research purposes. Ordinal type items seemed to be more useful than nominal. This suggests minor revisions. Also the other variables might be added, such as the extent to which there were administrative, space, or other obstacles impeding efforts. Items might also be added about the reward system for the innovative in the school. It would seem, however, that shortened, standardized instruments similar to the ATI, IEO and IET might be constructed by researchers and made available for the effective gathering of information.

TABLE B-5. Correlation Coefficients of Similar Individual Items on the Inventory of Educational Practices (by Schools).

	Pearson's r
Personal Usage vs Relative Use	.86
Attitude toward Rapidity of Change vs Attitude toward Innovation	.80
Communication within building vs to Community	.62
Attitude toward Technological vs Curriculum Innovations	.86
Influence of Administrators in Introducing vs Their Influence on Success of Innovations	.74

Exhibit B-4 — Inventory of Educational Practices (IEP)

General Directions: Each page contains a short paragraph that explains the topic of that page and indicates how you are to respond. An asterisk (*) serves to call your attention to any modification of the response procedure.

You should record all your answers in this booklet. The usual procedure is to darken the appropriate letter of the response category most indicative of your answer.

Example: How suitable for use of an innovation such as flexible scheduling are the physical facilities of your school?

A. Very

B. Quite
C. Moderately
D. Somewhat
E. Not at all

This choice indicates that in the respondent's estimation the physical facilities of his school are somewhat suitable for flexible scheduling.

I. SPREAD OF INFORMATION

The questions on this page refer to the means whereby information about innovations circulates in the school. Darken the appropriate letter indicative of your response to each question.

1. By what means do you get most of your information about innovations? Through:
   A. Formal course work
   B. Contact with others
   C. Reading
   D. Mass media: TV and radio
   E. In-service workshops

2. Which form of reading listed below provides you with the most information about innovations.
   A. Newspapers
   B. Official bulletins and news letters
   C. Professional literature
   D. Nonprofessional literature
   E. Commercial literature

3. Which form of contacts with others provides you with the most information about innovations? Contact with:
   A. Administrators in your school
   B. Teachers in your school
   C. Curriculum or media specialists within the school district
   D. Professionals other than (C) within the school district
   E. Professionals outside the school district

4. How effective within the building do you estimate school-originated information about innovations to be?
   A. Very effective
   B. Quite effective
   C. About equally effective and ineffective
   D. Quite ineffective
   E. Very ineffective

5. How much information does the school provide the community about the innovations that it is introducing?
   A. A great deal
   B. Considerable
   C. Moderate
   D. Slight
   E. None

6. How much has seeing the Kettering brochures *Taking Part in Secondary School Innovation* influenced your attitude toward innovation?
   A. A great deal
   B. Considerable

C. Moderate
D. Slight
E. None
F. Did not receive any brochure

II. AWARENESS

These questions concern the amount of information that you know about innovation in your school and in general. Darken the appropriate letter indicative of your response to each question.

1. Which statement best describes the extent of your formal training in the use of innovations in general over the past two years?
   A. No formal training
   B. One or more part-time, in-service workshops
   C. One or more full-time workshops of up to one week's duration
   D. One of more full-time workshops of up to two weeks' duration
   E. One or more courses of two weeks' duration or longer
2. Compared to other teachers in your school, where do you rank yourself in terms of the information that you possess about innovations?
   A. Very informed
   B. Quite informed
   C. About equally informed and equally uninformed
   D. Quite uninformed
   E. Very uninformed

Which of these innovations do you know are in use, or are planned for, in your school building?

Key to categories:
   Adopted: used on a widespread basis
   Experimental: used on a limited basis
   Planned: adoption within 3 years

	Use		Planned		
Curricular:	**Adopted**	**Experimental**	**Yes**	**No**	**Unfamiliar**
3. New English curricula	(A)	(B)	(C)	(D)	(E)
4. New Math curricula	(A)	(B)	(C)	(D)	(E)
5. New Science curricula	(A)	(B)	(C)	(D)	(E)
6. New Social Studies curricula	(A)	(B)	(C)	(D)	(E)
Technological:					
7. Closed-circuit TV	(A)	(B)	(C)	(D)	(E)
8. Independent study carrels with associated A-V equipment	(A)	(B)	(C)	(D)	(E)
9. Overhead projector	(A)	(B)	(C)	(D)	(E)
10. 8mm loop projector	(A)	(B)	(C)	(D)	(E)

11. How many of the above items (3 – 10) do you feel are suitable innovations for your school system?
    A. 7 – 8
    B. 5 – 6
    C. 3 – 4

D. 1 – 2

E. None of them

III. USAGE

This section asks you to estimate your own usage of innovations with groups or individuals. Darken the appropriate letter indicative of your response to each question.

1. How much use do you personally make of any curricular or technological innovation in your present position?
   A. A great deal
   B. Considerable
   C. Moderate
   D. Slight
   E. None

2. Compared to similar school professionals in general, how much use do you make of innovations?
   A. A great deal
   B. Considerable
   C. Moderate
   D. Slight
   E. None

3. Which of these technological innovations do you use the most?
   A. Overhead projector
   B. Closed-circuit TV
   C. 16mm projector
   D. 8mm loop projector
   E. Record player

4. Which of these organizations for instruction do you use the most?
   A. Nearly all group instruction
   B. Mainly groups with some individual instruction
   C. About equally group and equally individual instruction
   D. Some groups with mainly individual instruction
   E. Nearly all individual instruction

5. Ideally which one of these organizations for instruction would you like to use the most?
   A. Nearly all group instruction
   B. Mainly groups with some individual instruction
   C. About equally group and equally individual instruction
   D. Some groups with mainly individual instruction
   E. Nearly all individual instruction

IV. ATTITUDES

These questions ask you (a) to estimate the attitudes of various other groups toward innovation and (b) to indicate to what extent you personally would support innovation. Darken the appropriate letter indicative of your response to each question.

A. Estimates of the attitudes of others
   1. Which of the categories best describes the general attitude of the professional staff toward adoption of a curricular innovation?
      A. Very favorable

B.   Quite favorable

C.   About equally favorable and unfavorable

D.   Quite unfavorable

E.   Very unfavorable

2.   Which of the categories best describes the general attitude of the professional staff toward adoption of a technological innovation?

    A.   Very favorable

    B.   Quite favorable

    C.   About equally favorable and unfavorable

    D.   Quite unfavorable

    E.   Very unfavorable

3.   Which of the categories best describes the community's attitude toward innovation in its schools?

    A.   Very favorable

    B.   Quite favorable

    C.   About equally favorable and unfavorable

    D.   Quite unfavorable

    E.   Very unfavorable

B. Your own involvement

4.   In general which rate of educational change do you prefer?

    A.   Very rapid

    B.   Quite rapid

    C.   Moderately rapid

    D.   Quite gradual

    E.   Very gradual

5.   Which level of expenditure per pupil to defray the cost of innovations would you support?

    A.   A large increase

    B.   A slight increase

    C.   The same as now

    D.   A slight decrease

    E.   A large decrease

6.   If you had an opportunity to introduce an innovation and participate in a university-sponsored, in-service training program next year, would you like to do so?

    A.   Most definitely yes

    B.   Probably yes

    C.   Undecided

    D.   Probably no

    E.   Definitely no

7.   Which category best describes your own attitude toward the introduction of new ideas and techniques at the secondary school level?

    A.   Very favorable

    B.   Quite favorable

    C.   About equally favorable and unfavorable

    D.   Quite unfavorable

    E.   Very unfavorable

V. INFLUENCE

These questions ask your opinion as to which sources contribute to the process of innovation. Darken the appropriate letter indicative of your response to each question.

In general how much influence do you feel the following groups of professionals have in determining which innovations are introduced into your school?

1. Administrators
   A. A great deal
   B. Considerable
   C. Moderate
   D. Slight
   E. None
2. Faculty in the school
   A. A great deal
   B. Considerable
   C. Moderate
   D. Slight
   E. None
3. Innovative teachers
   A. A great deal
   B. Considerable
   C. Moderate
   D. Slight
   E. None

In general how much influence do you feel the following groups of professionals have in determining the *success* of an innovation?

4. Administrators
   A. A great deal
   B. Considerable
   C. Moderate
   D. Slight
   E. None
5. Faculty in the school
   A. A great deal
   B. Considerable
   C. Moderate
   D. Slight
   E. None
6. Innovative teachers
   A. A great deal
   B. Considerable
   C. Moderate
   D. Slight
   E. None
7. How much influence has the Kettering Project had on innovation within the school?
   A. A great deal
   B. Considerable
   C. Moderate
   D. Slight
   E. None
8. Which department in the school do you believe has been the most innovative during the past two years_____?

Inventory of Trust, Openness, and Adaptability — Cooperative Project in Educational Development (Norms, Do's and Don'ts, Form A-4 — COPED)

Description. This is one of the scales developed by Hilfiker (1969 as part of a COPED study). Ten of his twenty-six items were used: Measures of Trust (4), Openness (3), and Availability (3). The items inquire about specific things that a person might do or say about his school system. These are informal "Do's" or "Don'ts" that are not written in the school regulations, but serve as a kind of code. They indicate what people in the system should or should not do if they are to be accepted by others.

Subjects. Hilfiker administered the test to 585 professional school personnel in eight school systems. Factor analysis revealed that most of the variance of sixteen of the items could be accounted for by the factors listed above. The ten items used had the heaviest factor loadings. In the present study the COPED "norms" instrument was administered to 671 school professionals in the twenty-six control and eleven experimental schools.

Response Mode. The respondees were asked to give two answers to each item. First, they were asked what percentage of professionals in the building feel they should or should not do or say or think. They wrote in the percentage. Second, each was asked to blacken one of the spaces to indicate how he would feel (See Exhibit B-5).

Scoring: Each person has two scores:(1) how he views others in the system (it is scored, percent who should minus percent who should not); and (2) how he feels scored: should 3, indifferent, 2; should not, 1).

Reliability and Validity: Hilfiker presents no evidence on reliability other than that of the homogeneity implied by the factor analysis results. In the present study, the COPED variable showed — correlation coefficients of .49 to .60 with gain in faculty attitude. This indirectly suggests that the instrument is moderately reliable.

Comments. If the health of a system is a prerequisite for innovative progress, more research should be devoted to checking on the reliability and validity of available COPED type instruments. The COPED instrument shows some promise, as does the instrument, Evaluation of the School system by Employees (see Chapter XI). The latter, in addition to trustfulness, measures creativity, facing problems and development, which seemed to have discriminating power between school A and school B.

Exhibit B-5. The Instrument for Measuring Staff Openness,
Trust and Adaptiveness
(Using selected COPED items)

This page contains a list of unwritten do's and don'ts in the school. For each statement you are to estimate how many professionals in the building would feel that you should do it, and how many would feel that you should not do it (in terms of percentages). Then darken the appropriate letter indicative of your own feeling toward the behavior.

1. tell colleagues what you really think
   of their work   (A)   (B)   (C)   100%
2. try out new ways of doing things, even
   if it's uncertain how they will work out.   (A)   (B)   (C)   100%
3. ask others to tell you what they really
   think of your work.   (A)   (B)   (C)   100%
4. be skeptical about accepting unusual
   or "way out" ideas.   (A)   (B)   (C)   100%
5. keep your real thoughts and reactions
   to yourself, by and large.   (A)   (B)   (C)   100%
6. be skeptical about things, as a rule.   (A)   (B)   (C)   100%
7. point out other people's mistakes, to
   improve working effectiveness.   (A)   (B)   (C)   100%
8. avoid disagreement and conflict
   whenever possible.   (A)   (B)   (C)   100%
9. trust others not to take advantage
   of you.   (A)   (B)   (C)   100%
10. stick with the familiar way of doing
    things in one's work.   (A)   (B)   (C)   100%

Scoring key: (a) perception of others, SHOULD (+%), SHOULD NOT (−%), INDIFFERENT (0)

        (b) self-perception SHOULD (3), SHOULD NOT (2), INDIFFERENT (1)

        (c) Open., 1 (+), 3 (+), 5 (+), 7 (+), 8 (−); Trust, 6 (−), 9 (+); Adapt., 2 (+), 4 (−), 10 (−).

Instruments for Measuring Influences on Students
Inventory of Education Techniques (IET)

Description. This twenty-six item scale was developed by the project staff. It measures the extent to which students participated in three types of innovations "during the past week": (1) media; (2) new instructional techniques; (3) direct student participation (see Chapter 10).

Subjects. The instrument was administered to 1053 pupils in the twenty-six school districts who answered with respect to their use of innovations in all of their classes. It was administered to the same pupils twice (1968 and 1970).

Response Mode. Students answered each item by checking whether they "had" or "had not" or "were unaware that they had participated" in each activity.

Scoring. Each student is assigned three-part scores and a total score based on the number of yes's answered.

Reliability and Validity. Correlation coefficients between pre- and post-tests shows considerable change occurs and so give little indication of the reliability of the instrument. Those correlations are .39, −.17, and .02 and .33 for the three parts and total respectively. However, validity coefficients imply that the reliability must be at least .69. (See Table B-6.) The reliability coefficient of Part I is at least .65 and of Part III at least .57. These are the largest intercorrelations obtained between parts of the IET.

To obtain the "concurrent" validity coefficient, The IET total score (post-survey) was correlated with the teacher response as to his personal usage of innovation, (Item III-1, post-survey). The average "usage score" for each of the twenty-six schools was then calculated (1) based on student estimates (IET) and (2) on teacher estimates, Item III-1,(post-survey). The resulting validity coefficients between the two was .69. For the three parts, comparable validity coefficients were .75, .09 and .44. Evidently the teachers were not including the use of new instructional procedures (as defined by Part II of the IET) as part of their responses. They seemed to emphasize the use of media (see correlation with Part I of the IET.)

Comments. This instrument seems to have sufficient reliability and validity to be used for research programs to determine the impact of innovations in student image. Part I has the highest validity coefficient (.75).

Why were the validity coefficients for Parts II and III only .09 and .44? High coefficients were obtained with an alternate teacher usage rating (with pre-survey, .52 and with post-survey, .35). Thus it would seem that the teachers were not including independent study, team teaching and use of other new instructional procedures when making their responses to Item III-1 (personal use of innovations). They were emphasizing media.

TABLE B–6. Validity Coefficients for the Inventory of Educational Techniques Scale (Students' Report Post-Survey)

1. IET total vs. Teacher's Personal Use of Innovations (Self-Report)	.69
2. IET total vs. Usage (Multi-Choice) (Teachers' Judgment)	.37
3. IET total vs. Usage (Raters' Judgment of Usage in School)	.19

Exhibit B-6. Inventory of Educational Techniques

DIRECTIONS: The questions in this booklet ask you to recall, as best as you can, certain activities that may have taken place during school this week. There is no time limit, but you should not spend too much time on any one question. The answers you make should represent your own judgment, not someone elses'.

You may not be familiar with some of the equipment mentioned; in this case, merely check Unfamiliar. On the other hand, you may have worked with a piece of equipment, but are not sure of its name; you should check Uncertain and briefly describe the equipment.

A. During school hours this week, did you watch . . .

    1. any non-commercial motion-picture films shown on a 16mm projector?
        Yes (If Yes, during how many periods?)
        No
        Unfamiliar to me
        Uncertain. Explain:

2. a transparency shown on an overhead projector?
>   Yes (If Yes, during how many periods?)
>   No
>   Unfamiliar to me
>   Uncertain. Explain:

3. a filmstrip shown on a filmstrip machine?
>   Yes (If Yes, during how many periods?)
>   No
>   Unfamiliar to me
>   Uncertain. Explain:

4. a television program from an educational television station?
>   Yes (If Yes, during how many periods?)
>   No
>   Unfamiliar to me
>   Uncertain. Explain:

5. a television tape made by teachers and/or students in the school?
>   Yes (If Yes, during how many periods?)
>   No
>   Unfamiliar to me
>   Uncertain. Explain:

6. a loop film shown on an 8mm projector?
>   Yes (If Yes, during how many periods?)
>   No
>   Unfamiliar to me
>   Uncertain. Explain:

B. During school hours this week, did you see . . .

7. a micro-film reader (a machine to read microfilms such as the *New York Times* series)?
>   Yes (If Yes, how many different times?)
>   No
>   Unfamiliar to me
>   Uncertain. Explain:

8. a language master, or electric card flasher, or controlled reader, or any other machine that teaches reading?
>   Yes (If Yes, how many different times?)
>   No
>   Unfamiliar to me
>   Uncertain. Explain:

9. a teaching machine (a machine that tells you almost immediately whether your answer is correct or not)?
>   Yes (If Yes, how many different times?)
>   No
>   Unfamiliar to me
>   Uncertain. Explain:

10. an electronic desk calculator that you can program?
>   Yes (If Yes, how many different times?)
>   No
>   Unfamiliar to me
>   Uncertain. Explain:

103

11. an electronic computer?

Yes (If Yes, how many different times?)

No

Unfamiliar to me

Uncertain. Explain:

12. an independent study carrel equipped with electronic equipment such as earphones, a tape recorder, and a projector (other than a language lab)?

Yes (If Yes, how many different times?)

No

Unfamiliar to me

Uncertain. Explain:

C. During school hours this week, did . . .

13. your regular teacher work, in partnership, with another teacher to teach your class (team teaching)?

Yes Explain:

No

Uncertain

14. your teacher meet with your entire class at differently scheduled periods, then meet with it in small groups (Large-small group instruction)?

Yes Explain:

No

Uncertain

D. During school hours this week, did you . . .

15. watch, or listen to, any type of equipment not mentioned above?

Yes Explain:

No

Uncertain

16. yourself use any equipment not mentioned above?

Yes Explain:

No

Uncertain

17. yourself prepare any materials to use with any piece of equipment?

Yes Explain:

No

Uncertain

18. attend a class in a course that no teacher has taught in the school before this year (a course new to the school)?

Yes Explain:

No

Uncertain

19. work on an independent study project (a study project in which you work independently under a teacher's guidance without attending class)?

Yes Explain:

No

Uncertain

20. work with books, recordings, and related magazines in a section of the library equipped as a study area for a course (English, social studies, industrial arts study areas)?

Yes Explain:

No

Uncertain

E. In your opinion . . .
    21. would you prefer that next year   (Choose one)
        a.   most courses in the school remain pretty much as they are now?
        b.   most courses in the school change quite a bit?
        Explain your choice:

The answers I have given are as accurate as I can make them.

      Your signature

Please return this booklet to your homeroom teacher before the close of school. Thank you.

Inventory of Educational Opinions (IEO)

Description. This 56-item instrument was developed by Walberg. The items described dynamic aspects of the classes the student attends. Included are such aspects as friction among students, understanding of goals, favoritism and sufficiency of physical space. The fourteen categories of items are listed in Chapter 10.

Subjects. The inventory was administered to 998 of the same students in 1968 and again in 1970.

Response Mode. Students darken one of five choices for each item to indicate their perception of whether the item describes the situation in their classes. These students were those in the innovating teacher's class but were asked to include all the classes they attended.

Scoring. Each student received fourteen scores based on a 5, 4, 3, 2, 1 weighting of the classes from "Very true" to "Very false". All items were scored positively and the category title adjusted to indicate the direction of the scale.

Reliability and Validity. Evidence on the reliability of the instrument in the present study is obtained from the intercorrelation of the 14 parts. On the first scale the range of correlation coefficients is from .48 to .80. (Informality vs Non-Apathy, and Organization vs Diversity). The median highest correlation between parts is .65. Therefore, it would seem that the reliability of the typical part is at least .65. Also, factor analysis confirms the existence of twelve factors. This means that, as the author intended, there is greater homogeneity of items within, than between parts.

    Conclusions with respect to the validity of the instrument cannot be drawn from the present study. It has no measure of the same 14 variables drawn from different sources.

Comments. The instrument appears to be well-constructed. The content of the items seems to have face validity when compared to factor analysis results. The reliability of most of the fourteen parts seems to be at least .65. Validity information is lacking. However, this kind of an instrument is important for studies of innovation and change. Long-lasting innovations occur when they have an impact on and become part of the lives of the students. If students are convinced that their education is bettered by a new practice, they are apt to persuade parents, administrators and others to support the continuation of that new practice. As the process of student feedback gains in acceptance, and as responsible students gain more of a voice in how they are taught, the need for instruments of this kind will become more evident.

Exhibit B-7. Inventory of Educational Opinions

Directions: Each statement in this booklet describes some aspect of the classes you attend in this school. You are to decide how true or false each statement is. There are no right or wrong answers. You have to use your own best judgment.

Beside each statement there are five categories of possible answers.

Very True	Somewhat True	Undecided	Somewhat False	Very False
VT	ST	?	SF	VF

You are to read each statement and decide which one category best describes the question, then darken the abbreviation for that category. eg.

VT	ST	?	SF	VF

This means that the category Somewhat True is the answer to a statement. Judge every statement on how true or false it is in relation to what happens in your classes. Use the category Undecided as a last resort.

In my classes most students do not have a change to get to know what their classmates are really like.	VT	ST	?	SF	VF
Many of my classmates have little respect for other students' opinions.	VT	ST	?	SF	VF
Many students refuse to be separated from their small groups of friends in class.	VT	ST	?	SF	VF
Many of my classmates seem indifferent toward what happens in class.	VT	ST	?	SF	VF
Each student in my class enjoys the same privileges as everyone else.	VT	ST	?	SF	VF
Students who break classroom rules are severely, but justly, punished.	VT	ST	?	SF	VF
Many students in my classes enjoy doing work for their courses.	VT	ST	?	SF	VF
In my classes there is plenty of time for most students to cover the assigned work.	VT	ST	?	SF	VF
Most classes I attend are easy for the average students in them.	VT	ST	?	SF	VF
Most students in my classes have little notion of what their classes are supposed to accomplish.	VT	ST	?	SF	VF
In my classes the students do not share in making the decisions about matters that directly concern them.	VT	ST	?	SF	VF
There are long stretches of time during which my classes do nothing of value for the students.	VT	ST	?	SF	VF
In my classes the students show that they have many interests.	VT	ST	?	SF	VF
There is enough space in the classrooms for groups of 8 – 10 students to work separately.	VT	ST	?	SF	VF
The students in my classes trust each other well enough to show what kind of persons they really are.	VT	ST	?	SF	VF
There are bad feelings among groups of students that tend to interfere with classroom activities.	VT	ST	?	SF	VF
Most students work well only with a certain few classmates.	VT	ST	?	SF	VF

Most students want to feel that their class as a whole is making progress in learning.	VT	ST	?	SF	VF
The better-liked students in my classes get special privileges.	VT	ST	?	SF	VF
The classes I am in have strict rules to follow.	VT	ST	?	SF	VF
Many students detest the work in their classes.	VT	ST	?	SF	VF
Most of my classmates have difficulty keeping up with the assigned work.	VT	ST	?	SF	VF
The classes I attend are difficult even for the average students in them.	VT	ST	?	SF	VF
Each of my classes has specific goals that I understand.	VT	ST	?	SF	VF
Students in my classes help make decisions in matters that affect them.	VT	ST	?	SF	VF
The work assignments made in my classes are clearly organized.	VT	ST	?	SF	VF
Many of my classmates reveal in class that they have a wide range of worthwhile interests.	VT	ST	?	SF	VF
Most classrooms have movable worktables and chairs.	VT	ST	?	SF	VF
In my classes most students do not know each others' first names.	VT	ST	?	SF	VF
Quite a few students in my classes start serious quarrels with their classmates.	VT	ST	?	SF	VF
Some groups of students work together regardless of what their classmates are doing.	VT	ST	?	SF	VF
Many students sincerely want their classes to be successful.	VT	ST	?	SF	VF
Certain students in my classes receive more special favors than the others do.	VT	ST	?	SF	VF
Most of the classes I attend are casual with only a few school-wide rules to observe.	VT	ST	?	SF	VF
The majority of my classmates look forward to going to class.	VT	ST	?	SF	VF
The average student does not get the class time to finish his/her work in my courses.	VT	ST	?	SF	VF
The better students in my classes consider their courses to be difficult.	VT	ST	?	SF	VF
Nearly every student is trying to reach the goals set for his/her classes.	VT	ST	?	SF	VF
The students have little share in making the class rules that directly concern how they behave.	VT	ST	?	SF	VF
The work that my classes have to do is not organized well.	VT	ST	?	SF	VF

New educational practices included individualized instruction.

Thirty-one innovating teachers introduced innovations and change.

APPENDIX C

DESCRIPTIONS OF THIRTY-ONE INNOVATIVE PROJECTS
CONDUCTED IN THE EXPERIMENTAL SCHOOLS

Contents

An Innovating teacher arranging a Mathematics laboratory.

A computer terminal provides student motivation and instruction.

Innovation 1: (a) Large-Group, Small-Group Instruction; (b) Multi-Media; (c) an Examination of Small Groups organized on Heterogeneous and Homogeneous Basis; (d) stresses of Fenton materials as an approach to the new Social Studies.

Teacher: Mr. Michael Sewall   Grade: Tenth

School: Sauquoit Valley Central School   Length of Program: One year

RATIONALE FOR INNOVATION

The desire on the part of the teacher to experiment with large group and small group instruction grew out of past difficulties in trying to cope with individual differences in interest and ability while working with regular size classes. It was felt that the use of small group instruction would accomplish two objectives: (1) enable the teacher to individualize instruction to a much greater extent by making the identification of individual differences easier and the designing appropriate learning activities; (2) increase student interaction in subject matter related discussions by forming groups small enough (10 − 12) so that the tendency of domination by the teacher or a few students common in regular size classes is removed. The large group sessions were seen as a time for the efficient use of media presentations, demonstrations, panels, guests to the schools, and teacher lectures. Some objectives of the social studies could best be accomplished in the setting of large group instruction, while others, perhaps the most important objectives, demanded small group instructions. Further, the teacher felt that the goal of developing the skills and attitudes necessary for individual study could best be met from the vantage point provided in small groups. A considerable amount of time was spent in preparing for this project, identifying objectives and classifying the best means (large group, small group, independent study programs) for accomplishing them.

While working on revising the curriculum it became apparent that help could be provided in accomplishing the objectives by the tools of the newer media: large group presentations could be greatly supplemented by the use of commercial transparencies, film strips, tapes, slides, movies and by teacher prepared materials as well. Small groups used these tools as resources for independent and group work, a stimulus for discussion, and explanations needing constant participatory feedback. The teacher also decided to experiment with curriculum materials being published as a result of the work of Edwin Fenton as a very viable approach to the teacher's understanding of the objectives of the New Social Studies.

HARDWARE

1. Film strip projector.   2. 2 Film strip previewers for students use
3.   Kodak Ektagraphic Visual-Maker for slide production
4.   3 Panasonic cassette tape recorders and headsets
5.   Slide projector
6.   Overhead projector
7.   Record player
8.   Wall screen
9.   16mm movie projector

Note: This equipment was provided by the project and supplemented by already existing equipment in the school.

CLASSROOM ACTIVITIES

The project covered an entire year and therefore included a great variety of activities. The activities listed below are characteristic and representative of approaches tried by the teacher:

1. Large group sessions met twice a week and were primarily devoted to media presentations (movies, film strips, slides, transparencies and appropriate narrations), teacher lectures, student presentations, and discussions by guests to the school. A good example of guest discussions was the pair of representatives giving views on the Middle East Crisis: one from the Jewish community in Utica, one from the Arab community. At the request of students early in the school year, time was allowed at the end of all large group sessions for student reaction and questions.

   All large group sessions were taped and made available with appropriate slides, film strips, etc. for students missing the session or wishing to review. The recorder used (Panasonic cassette tape recorder) also served the function of a loudspeaker in the auditorium.

2. Small group sessions were considered the main part of the program and also met twice a week with 10 – 12 students as the average class size. Student interaction with other students and the teacher was stressed. In these sessions the objective of the teacher was to identify individual differences in ability and interest, and to select readings and design learning activities according to these differences. Group and individual student projects also grew out of the sessions.

   Characteristic activities in small group sessions included: (a) reactions to large group presentations; (b) discussion of readings assigned to the particular group, which often varied in difficulty even within one small group; (c) individual and group work on research projects; (d) use of media presentations which required more feedback than possible in large groups; (e) use of the Follet Basic Learning Program with a few, slower students and (f) use of the Fenton readings and audio-visual materials.

3. Individual and Group research projects grew out of small group sessions and were assigned according to the interests of the students involved. Although many of these individual study projects were of a more traditional type, many students took advantage of the fact that the media tools being used by the teacher were also at their disposal. A project resulting from the philosophy of following the interest of students and allowing for a variety of media was done by a group of boys involved in a BOCES auto-mechanic program, consisting of print, slides, and taped interviews concerning the impact of the auto on our country. Another consisted of slides, taped narration, poetry, and music in a conceptual interpretation of the causes of unrest in our society today. In both cases much actual research of the more traditional type had to be done in conjunction with the project, while the method of expression allowed for greater creativity, interest, and use of resources in the community.

OBSERVED DIFFUSION ON INNOVATION

Several opportunities for diffusion of the ideas of this project were given the teacher:

1. The project was covered by the Utica newspaper resulting in two articles.
2. The teacher took part in a presentation on innovations in social studies at the New York State Council for the Social Studies meeting in New York City.
3. Several teachers from outside the school district visited classes being conducted by the project teacher.
4. Several teachers from the district were frequent visitors to the classes and expressed interest through conversations throughout the year. The newer media made available for the project were in frequent circulation.

TEACHER EVALUATION

1. The large group sessions were of limited success. Twice a week was considered too much for both teacher and students and might better be reduced to once a week. These sessions did provide for efficient use of media presentations (such as movies), guests to the school, and certain lectures by the teacher. Students asked for more time to react in the large groups and this was provided.

2. Small group sessions were a great success, as reported by the teacher and substantiated by a series of evaluation forms filled out by students during the year for the teacher. The teacher felt better able to deal with individual differences than in his past experiences with regular classes of $20-30$ students. Student involvement and participation were judged significantly higher.

3. The rigid and uniform periods of instructional time during the school day placed restraints on the program.

4. The curriculum materials published under the general editorship of Edwin Fenton received praise from the teacher. These materials have to be supplemented or modified according to the type of student, but he felt they provided for the type of inquiry within the range of abilities of his students. The unit "An Introduction to the Study of History" was especially well received with the teacher noting numerous cases of carry-over within his own class and in other disciplines. The inquiry approach, clearly stated objectives, and ease in modifying the program to meet individual differences were all considered to be advantages of the program.

5. The group and individual projects which used a variety of media seemed to create more interest during the past year than in other years, on the part of those involved and in other students during presentations to the class.

6. The need for greater paraprofessional help became apparent as the teacher attempted to individualize instruction.

   Note: A bibliography of materials used is available from the Kettering Project, Colgate University.

Innovation 2: **Development and Implementation of a unit of study on "Race Relations In America"; Multi-Media approaches to learning; use of Group and Independent study programs.**

Teacher: Mrs. Ethel B. Hoag   Grade: Twelfth

School: Greene Central School   Length of Program: Three Months

RATIONALE FOR INNOVATION

The desire for the project grew out of several related observations made by the teacher:

1. The important role the social studies can and should play in examining current societal problems;

2. The high interest level and relevancy of the topic for students but, at the same time, lack of knowledge of current social science research on the topic;

3. The need for students to reflect upon, through rational means, the values, attitudes, and data they have accumulated in their life experiences;

4. The existence of racial conflicts, problems, and misconceptions even in small white communities;

5. The topic naturally lent itself very well to the overall social studies objectives the teacher felt important: having students become more aware of themselves and others by providing an environment in which they can reflect upon values and attitudes, examine the process by which they are arrived at, and participate in rational discussion and research aimed at a better understanding of them.

Along with the development of the specific topic, the project attempted to experiment with various types of learning activities and techniques which followed the inquiry, or investigation-oriented type of approach to the social studies and made provisions for individual differences in ability and interest. In this context, the role of the teacher was seen as being a motivator, resource person, sometimes an instigator, and always a fellow inquirer. The attitudes of the teacher were expressed freely in the course of discussions as expressions of just one more frame of reference and were closely examined accordingly. Careful attention was given to insuring student understanding of the teacher's role and her expectations: examination of, rather than compliance to, values and attitudes expressed in class. Finally, it was felt that much of the "canned" material being provided commercially on this topic missed much of current reality by providing only the "contributions of the black" approach, by not being based on recent social science research, and by not being conducive to the inquiry approach to the social studies. Attempts were made to exclude such material during time set aside for previewing.

HARDWARE

1. 4 Cassette tape recorders with headsets
2. Reel to reel type tape recorder
3. 16mm movie projector
4. Record player
5. 5 individual filmstrip previewers
6. Video tape recording system
7. 2 combined sound-filmstrip units
8. Several individual study carrels

CLASSROOM ACTIVITIES

Activities for this unit were selected or designed, based upon a commitment to the philosophy of the inquiry approach to the social studies. Some of the activities used, and listed below, were unplanned, student initiated explorations. The guidelines used in selecting curriculum materials to be utilized included: the relevancy to the student and motivational appeal; the need for a variety of material to meet individual ability and interest differences; the desire to provide a variety of interpretations for students to consider; and the goal of providing material which reflected current research of the social sciences.

As a result of experiences gained during this project, the following activities were selected as being particularly helpful in meeting the objectives of this topic:

1. Readings – A wide variety of readings were made available to the class. Only *Crisis in Black and White* was mandatory reading for all students; the other printed material being used according to research projects selected by students within the guidelines set down in "Topics for Inquiry". The Silberman book was used to give a common point of reference for all students in order to focus attention and discussions, and as a means of initiating further research into problems raised in the book.

2. Other Curriculum Materials – A variety of audio-visual materials (audiotapes, film strips, records, etc.) were included. These materials were used for the most part on an individual or small group basis. Several individual study carrels were located in the back of the classroom for this purpose and were available to students for research purposes at any time during the school day.

3. Independent and Group Study – Students were allowed to follow personal interests within the very general outline structure predetermined by the teacher and based upon the availability of materials (i.e., Black Poetry, the Nature of

112

Prejudice, Identity, . . .). During time set aside for such work the teacher was able to work intensively on an individual and group basis with students. Students were asked to report back to class and lead discussions which resulted.

4. Original Research — As part of the independent and group study projects students were encouraged to collect and examine information concerning their topics locally, with the help of the teacher questionnaires which were circulated within the school and community. Interviews were also conducted. Students were asked to critically examine the techniques of their research projects as well as the content, and to compare findings to more sophisticated studies.

5. Use of Outside Resource People — A number of people were invited into the classroom to provide for exposure to and interaction with blacks, an opportunity denied students in the past due their location and type of community. Visitors included representatives of the Binghamton Urban League and college students, providing a wide range of backgrounds. The students felt this to be one of the most important parts of the program; and the visitors remarked at the background the students obviously had as shown by the types of questions and discussions.

6. Field Trips — As part of an inquiry into the poverty of many Negroes a field trip to a black ghetto of a nearby city is recommended. This is made more meaningful if provision can be made for interviews with people associated with such organizations as an Urban League.

7. Movies — Movies played a special role in the development of this unit: as a means of supplementing visitors to the class and field work in making up for the lack of exposure and interaction with blacks; as a means of introducing various interpretations concerned with the topic, and as a stimulation for class discussions. The movies were selected for their interpretive value and open-endedness. It might be noted that such movies are the exception, with most of the currently commercial presentations available to teachers being expository in nature.

8. Class Discussions — The entire class met as a whole often during the unit for several specific purposes. At this time discussion was carried on resulting from: (a) movie presentations; (b) individual and group reports on research; (c) outside resource people; (d) items recently in the news; (e) and questions arising from students, raised by the teacher, or originating from the basic reading, *Crisis in Black and White*. These discussions were open and frank, with students referring to their research and exposing areas for future study. As the unit progressed students called for more such sessions to be held as a means of exploring individual and group values and attitudes. Rather than the traditional "teacher-teaching, student-learning" situation this might better be described as both teacher and students playing the roles of teacher and learner.

9. Fish Bowl Techniques — The "fish bowl design for discussion" ("Today's Education": *NEA Journal*, Sept. 1968) can very effectively be applied to such controversial topics as race relations. The technique itself involves having several students discuss an issue sitting in an inner circle, while the rest of the class listens to the interaction from an outer circle. The objectives are to involve the whole class in some meaningful way and to focus attention on specific, predetermined factors. The technique takes into consideration the fact that most discussions are dominated by a few, especially interested or

knowledgable students by allowing a few to engage in the initial interaction, selected on a certain criteria such as interest. The rest of the class is involved by giving them specific assignments, such as looking for unsupported statements (several individual assignments can be given to the group in the outer circle). At the conclusion of the discussion the outer circle contributes both on the subject of the discussion and observations of the process of the discussion.

TOPICS FOR INQUIRY

I. RACE

1. What is a good definition of race?
2. Are races "equal"?
3. How did racism start in a country which valued freedom and equality?
4. When did segregation begin in America? What kind of support did it receive from American institutions?
5. When, if ever, is it appropriate to use race as a basis for making private and public decisions?

II. IDENTITY OF THE RACES

1. What is it like to be black?
2. What factors play a significant role in establishing one's identity? What part does environment play?
3. Is it harder to be black than a member of any other minority?
4. Is the American Negro like the Negro in other countries?
5. If slavery existed in most civilized societies, why did it create a harder race problem for the United States?
6. How does it feel to be white in a racist society? Should white people have "guilt"?

III. PREJUDICE

1. Are students of Greene Central School prejudiced? Are people of our community white racists?
2. What is prejudice? How is it acquired?
3. What part do personality, group tensions and sterotyping play in the development of prejudice?
4. Is our view of the Negro a real one?
5. How can prejudice be reduced?
6. Does legislation play a role in the reduction of conflict? Can and should the government guarantee each individual a sense of worth and pride?

IV. THE ROAD TO EQUALITY

1. What level of culture has the Negro achieved in America?
2. What kind of progress has been made in American history toward the achievement of racial equality? By whom?
3. What is the right road to equality for the American Negro today? Which is the best answer?
4. Which of the Negro leaders today could you follow? Which will the Negro follow?
5. Is "equality and justice" more important than "law and order"? Can we simultaneously value social cohesion and minority rights?

V. THE ROLE OF INSTITUTIONS ALONG THE ROAD TO EQUALITY

1. Which institution in our society has the most to offer the Negro — the government, school, church, industry or the family? Are they adequate to meet current needs?
2. How can the environment of the ghetto be transformed?

3. What should be the role of the school? Are segregated or integrated schools better and for whom?
4. Can children of mixed marriages face the problem? Can a strong family provide the necessary support?
5. How can we broaden the base of interested people of good will who are willing to give up some of their own identity to eradicate racism?

OBSERVED DIFFUSION

Diffusion of the innovation through a number of means was noted by the teacher: several area schools contacted or visited the teacher during the year asking for help in developing similar programs of study; newspaper articles were written on her project, with especially good coverage from a Binghamton paper; contact was made with the Binghamton Urban League, an organization which provided assistance and expressed great interest; student teachers in the school visited the classroom and expressed interest in both the content and methods employed in the project; several other teachers in the school became very acquainted with the project and borrowed materials; a larger number of pupils signed up for the course than ever before, perhaps as a result of the project.

TEACHER EVALUATION

Several observations were made by the teacher at the conclusion of the project concerning successes and limitations:
1. The inquiry approach seemed especially well suited for such a controversial topic. Students were asked to draw their own conclusions based upon interaction with other students, discussions with the teacher and outside visitors, and from examination of a variety of interpretive analysis provided by the printed and audio-visual curriculum materials. It was felt that the goal of the social studies of helping develop critical, rational, decision-making citizens was furthered. At the same time the role of the teacher is seen more clearly as it should be: a resource rather than a propagandizer for a particular position. By providing a variety of materials and subtopics the individual differences in ability and interest were also taken into consideration.
2. Most interest was generated during and following live encounters with visitors to the classroom, and in conducting and critically examining original research by students on the local situation.
3. The conventional 45-minute periods were too rigid and confining.
4. Several cautious observations were made concerning behavorial changes of the students in relation to the topic: students came to understand the extent and complexity of the problem of race relations in the U.S.; they gained new conceptual tools from the social sciences to examine the subject; class interaction, visitors and interpretive works enabled students to view and examine various sides of a number of arguments in relation to the topic.
5. Independent and group study using various print and audio-visual materials was fruitful in creating motivation, allowing for individual interests and exposing students to a greater variety of subtopics.

Note: An extensive bibliography of materials used during this program is available from the Kettering Project, Colgate University.

Innovation 3: Development of methods and Techniques which permit more individualization of instruction, with special emphasis on the slower learner.

Teacher: Mr. Bruce Webster   Grade: Ninth
School: Morrisville-Eaton Central School   Length of Program: Two Months

RATIONALE FOR INNOVATION

The members of the social studies department met several times prior to the beginning of the project in an effort to identify major problems and goals of the department. As a result of these meetings they agreed that the goal of the project would be an attempt to individualize instruction to a much greater extent within their classrooms. Special emphasis, they felt, should be placed on the average and slower learner. The wide range of abilities and interests within each class was examined and discussed by the department members, and was seen as a factor demanding greater individualized attention than the more traditional group oriented instruction, in this case.

The project period was a time for experimenting with various methods and techniques which might facilitate individualization. One teacher was selected to act as demonstration teacher, with the other members of the department acting in supporting roles. Several important steps were then taken: (1) the reading specialist and guidance department were asked and subsequently agreed to be members of the departmental team; (2) a series of tests (Culture Fair I.Q., Achievement, Reading and Motivation-Interest) was given and added to existing test results; (3) media were selected which would help in the process of individualizing; and (4) a variety of curriculum materials were selected. The selection of curriculum materials of readings and the Communist World which were suitable for the various reading levels of the class involved. Other curriculum materials (slides, tapes, film strips, etc.) were also selected on the levels of difficulty corresponding to the range of abilities within the class.

HARDWARE

The following equipment was provided by the Kettering Project to supplement existing equipment:

1. Record player
2. Slide projector
3. Wall screen
4. 5 Panasonic cassette tape recorders with headsets
5. Kodak Ektagraphic Visual-Maker for teacher and student slide projection
6. Overhead projector
7. Film strip previewers

Note: The Kettering Project also supplied commercially prepared tapes, film strips, slides, records and transparencies, and provided ample materials for teacher and student prepared audio-visual aids.

CLASSROOM ACTIVITIES

The teacher initially worked out the objectives of the project unit and ordered curriculum materials accordingly. With the help of the rest of the social studies department, the reading specialist, the guidance department and the Kettering staff, the teacher attempted to obtain materials which varied according to the individual differences in ability and interest within his class. Several themes were characteristic of the project:

1. Small groups of students were identified through various tests and teacher judgment who had similar learning problems (e.g. reading) and interests. A lot of time during the project was spent with these groups working and discussing selected topics. Readings and audio-visual materials were assigned according to the general ability of the group and was even varied within each group. The teacher acted as motivator, facilitator and resource person for these groups and worked especially closely with slower students. Identification of individual problems seemed much easier in this setting.

2. Several of the students were identified as having serious reading problems and were re-assigned at scheduled intervals during the project to work with the reading specialist.
3. Individuals had a chance to work independently due to the variety of curriculum materials available and media selected for its capability to be used on an individual basis.
4. Presentations were made by the individual groups concerning the findings, discussions, techniques, and interpretations encountered. They, in turn, were discussed by the entire class. The groups had all the equipment provided by the project at their disposal for this purpose and learned to use these tools effectively. It was felt that this method of presentation helped to overcome fears students had as a result of past experiences of failure associated with work which was only print oriented.
5. Students frequently used the resources of the library during the project unit in the teacher's attempt to build library, reading, and research skills.
6. Teacher presentations to the entire class were greatly reduced as compared to the pre-project period, but took place at selected times according to the objectives worked out by the teacher, as a means of coordinating and motivating the groups. Most of the teacher's time was spent facilitating group work and discussion.

OBSERVED DIFFUSION

The ideas of the project were developed through the cooperative efforts of the entire social studies department of the school and implemented initially through the use of a demonstration teacher. As a result, there existed a continuous flow of communication and diffusion within the department during the project. As a direct consequence of the project, the department volunteered to work closely with Colgate University during the following year in a project aimed at examining the objectives of the social studies and experimenting with means of implementation.

TEACHER EVALUATION

The teacher made a series of observations concerning the attempt of the project to increase individualization of instruction in the regular class setting:

1. The design of the project, calling for departmental cooperation and the use of a demonstration teacher, helped to draw the department together and focus their attention on the goals of the social studies.
2. The idea and value of an effective testing program and cooperation with experts within the school (such as the reading specialist) were considered an important part of the project and provided the setting for similar experiences in the future.
3. The teacher considered the continuous regrouping of students within the classroom to be a tenable way to increase individualization. Differences in ability and interest could more easily be identified in this setting although the teacher felt that several small groups in the regular class setting might better be replaced by small groups meeting independently under large group-small group design.
4. As a result of the grouping of students the teacher was able to spend more time with the slower students, helping them gain direction in their work and facilitating interaction. The better students were more often able to assume the role of an independent inquirer.
5. The media provided by the project allowed the teacher to spend more time with students on analysis and evaluation of materials and less time in formal

presentations. The attempt to acquire curriculum materials (audio-visual and printed) which could account for individual differences was a partial success and pointed out areas of needed material for the future.

6. Each group project showed an increase in proficiency of group work and showed quantitative improvement. Interaction within the groups on matters of values and interpretation increased, and increased attention on the process of inquiry was evident.

7. The presentations of the smaller groups and individuals to the whole class concerning the work done did not gain the attention of most students and might better be changed or eliminated.

Innovation 4: (1) Use of various techniques (such as Bales' "Interaction Process Analysis") by students in task oriented situations for understanding and improving interaction within the classroom. (2) Applications of cassette tape recorders in social studies classroom, mainly for gathering information from primary sources.

Teacher: Mr. Edwin Ermlich   Grade: Twelfth
School: Bainbridge-Guilford Central School   Length of Program: One Semester

RATIONALE FOR INNOVATION

The teacher was involved in a 12th grade social studies course, "Problems of Democracy". In this course two objectives were considered of paramount importance: (1) meaningful interaction by the class on issues raised, and (2) the gathering of primary source information. The project was designed to attempt to satisfy both objectives.

As far as the first objective is concerned (that of establishing meaningful interaction) the teacher felt that most students lacked both an understanding of the value of group work and interaction, as well as the skills of interaction necessary for meaningful group exploration is inherent in the New Social Studies, it was also observed that little, if anything, has been done in the past to develop such understandings and skills expected of students.

The objective (the gathering of primary source material) involved the identification, classification, and discussion of various points of view and support evidence concerning topics raised during the course. The teacher hoped students would take advantage of such various resources as people in the community, other teachers, peers, TV, radio, and lectures in nearby colleges, as well as the more traditional sources provided by the teacher and the library. It was observed that many of these resources went unattended and that to insure the investigation orientation of the class steps should be taken to facilitate the collection of such data.

HARDWARE

1. 30 Panasonic cassette tape recorders and cassette tapes
2. 30 Individual Telex head sets

CLASSROOM ACTIVITIES

Several activities were employed in an attempt to satisfy the objectives of helping students develop an understanding of the process of group interaction and the development of skills needed for meaningful interaction within a group:

1. In order to have students begin to understand and examine the problems and potentials of group interaction such decision-making exercises as "Last on the Moon" was used (see *Today's Education,* NEA Journal, February 1969).

At the conclusion of such exercises students were directed toward several questions: Why did groups do better than individuals? How were group decisions arrived at? Were all the resources of each group used to the fullest extent?

2. The main activity during the project involved having students work in groups of six, discussing and working on issues raised during the regular class. In this task-oriented situation students would tape the discussion and then individually replay the tapes, and using Bales' Interaction Process Analysis derive a "profile" of the group's discussion. This was done over a period of several weeks, one day a week, with the Bales' categories usually being compiled as a homework assignment. The group would then spend a part of the next class period examining and discussing the process of the discussion which had taken place, failures and successes of the group's interaction, and explore ways to improve the process — all with the help of the teacher.

This procedure had the advantages of being able to look at the interaction process in an objective and meaningful way, keeping social studies oriented, being easy for students to understand, and not time consuming. The twelve categories of Bales' follow:

1. Shows solidarity, raises other's status, gives help, reward
2. Shows tension release, jokes, laughs, shows satisfaction
3. Agrees, shows passive acceptance, understands, concurs, compiles
4. Gives suggestion, direction implying autonomy for others
5. Gives opinion, evaluation, analysis, expresses feeling, wish
6. Gives orientation, information, repetition, confirmation
7. Asks for orientation, information, repetition, confirmation
8. Asks for opinion, evaluation analysis, expression of feeling
9. Asks for suggestion, direction, possible ways of action
10. Disagrees, shows passive rejection, formality, withholds help
11. Shows tension, asks for help, withdraws out of field
12. Shows antagonism, deflates others' status, defends or asserts self

3. Another recommended activity for helping students view the process of group interaction, as well as the content, is utilization of the "Fishbowl Technique" (as reported in *"Today's Education"*, NEA Journal, September 1968). Students form two circles of desks: an inner circle of several students assigned to discuss a problem raised in the study of social studies, and an outer circle comprised of the rest of the class and assigned to observe the discussion for certain elements, both process and content oriented. Discussion by the entire class following the initial interaction of the inner circle can then zero in on the way the small group functioned.

The second objective of the project was to facilitate the collection of primary and secondary resources which pertained to issues raised in the "Problems of Democracy" course. Although there exist a number of possible approaches that satisfy this objective, the project put emphasis on the portable cassette tape recorder as a tool. A bank of recorders and tapes was made available to students to use both for teacher directed and student initiated projects. A variety of applications were found successful:

1. Interviews were conducted by students with resource people within the community who could not be live guests in the classroom because of other time commitments. Examples of this approach included interviews with doctors in the subject of the influence of the news media on our population. These tapes were played back to the entire class and provided a larger frame of reference for the topic under consideration.
2. Several students used the tape recorder on an individual basis for collecting informational data and opinions for use in term papers, and used the tapes to

help in presentations of findings to the class.

3. Both the teacher and individual students used tapes taken from TV and radio programs to stimulate, initiate, and supplement discussion on a variety of topics of concern in the course.

4. Lectures by guests to the school and controversial people visiting nearby colleges were taped in certain cases with selected parts played back for thoughtful analysis and discussion.

OBSERVED DIFFUSION

The teacher noted no diffusion to the extent of actual implementation of the idea of helping students understand and develop skills involved in the group process. However, many teachers were interested in the project and discussed the ideas with the project teacher.

There were several teachers interested in the application of the cassette tape recorder in education, and different applications were made by these teachers in their own classes. Also, students within the project teacher's classroom became accustomed to viewing the recorder as another available tool and by the end of the year were using them in a variety of ways.

TEACHER EVALUATION

The teacher felt that several observations could be made regarding the project's attempt to help students understand and more efficiently participate in groups: students did focus their attention on the process of group work, as well as on content, as evidenced by the number of times the subject was brought up other than in planned sessions; students verbalized the discovery of various roles being played by individuals and potential resources within the groups; interaction seemed more open and more productive toward the end of the project, with a greater range of participants. Also, the teacher observed that students seemed better able to handle criticism from peers much more easily in the smaller groups than when the class met as an entire body. No trouble was encountered as far as learning the various techniques (Bales' NEA Interaction ideas) was concerned.

On the negative side, it was felt that the project could have been handled more efficiently if classes were originally assigned on a small group basis rather than forming them in a regular classroom setting. Furthermore, no firm and final conclusions can be drawn as to the effectiveness of any one of the techniques used due to a lack of a large enough population involved to form sufficient control groups. The use of the portable cassette tape recorder as a means of collecting information from primary sources was quite successful and opened up avenues of information heretofore untapped.

Innovation 5: Multi-Media approaches to the Social Studies.

Teacher: Mr. Paul Enea   Grade: Seventh

School: Chadwicks Union Free School   Length of Program: One Semester

RATIONALE FOR INNOVATION

The teacher listed several reasons in his original proposal to the Kettering Project for undertaking this particular project. Included were:

1. The need to investigate commercially prepared curriculum materials (tapes, slides, etc.) in order to enrich current printed materials and possibly aid the teacher in meeting the heavy work load common to most small schools;

2. Learn techniques of producing teacher-made materials;

3. Investigate new media not available to personnel at the school at that time;

4. Acquire needed experience in order to make recommendations for the multi-media learning center.

HARDWARE

1. 1 Slide projector
2. 1 Film strip projector
3. 4 Panasonic cassette tape recorders with individual headsets
4. 1 Kodak Ekagraphic Visual-Maker for teacher and student slide production
5. 2 Film strip previewers
6. 2 Slide previewers
7. 1 Classroom record player
8. 1 Overhead projector
9. 1 Wall screen

Note: The Kettering Project also supplemented existing school inventories of appropriate curriculum materials: commercially prepared tape, film, slides, film strips, transparencies, and printed materials. Consultation was provided in the preparation of teacher-made materials.

CLASSROOM ACTIVITIES

Many of the activities conducted during the project semester stressed the goal of student involvement through the creative and motivational potential of the newer media. Selected examples of these activities included:

1. Student production of curriculum related slides   For example, in preparing for a unit on architectural designs characteristic of N.Y. State and the local area, students took slides and conducted research on buildings in their own area and in nearby Utica for presentation to the class.

2. Student and teacher production of slide-tape presentations — A number of such presentations were worked out by the seventh graders including one outstanding conceptual interpretation of war using slides taken from various photographs during the Hitler era accompanied by interpretive music and narration using the visual maker and cassette tape recorder.

3. Commercially prepared materials — A fairly substantial inventory of purchased curriculum materials was provided (tapes, records, film strips, etc.). These materials were utilized mainly as a resource for student projects and presentations, but also in connection with presentations by the teacher. All such material and appropriate equipment could be used during any free time of the student or taken home.

4. Aid for substitute teachers — On a few occasions the teacher was unable to meet with his classes but provided for this by directing both the class and substitute through various media presentations, making explanations on an audio tape, and raising questions for class consideration.

5. Developing student skills in note taking — The teacher felt that one of the problems general to most seventh graders revolved around their lack of ability to take meaningful class and research notes. An attempt was made to meet this problem by having the teacher take example notes during his own presentations and during student reports, using the overhead projector.

OBSERVED DIFFUSION

Several avenues of diffusion were observed by the teacher. A multi-media presentation was made to the local PTA as an example to them of the potential of the media in education. Examples of the work being done by the teacher and his classes were presented to a general meeting of the school faculty. The teacher further noted that interest in the activities he was carrying on in his classroom as the project progressed. This was evidenced by increased use of the project ideas and equipment by other teachers in the school and students from other classes.

121

TEACHER EVALUATION

The teacher concluded that the project with the use of a variety of media, was beneficial for both himself and his students but pointed to space and time needs as problems which would have to be considered in following years. The goal of using media on a student-involvement basis was facilitated by the fact that the equipment provided required very little training of students and exhibited durability.

Innovation 6: Combined application of videotape recorder. Flanders interaction analysis, and peer group observations with the objective of teacher improvement.

Teachers: New York Mills Social Studies
Department (Mr. Richard Dunn)

School: New York Mills Central School
Grade: Seventh through Twelfth
Length of Program: This project was
in the development stage during
the action phase of the Kettering Project

RATIONALE FOR INNOVATION

The planned innovation was an attempt to coordinate and integrate three different methods which have been used independently by other schools and teacher-training institutions: Flanders Interaction Analysis; the V.T.R.; and peer group observations.

The Flanders System was selected to resolve the complexity and countless variables found in the teaching-learning process. The system places into ten categories verbal behavior or teachers and students on the assumption that an objective assessment of verbal behavior in a classroom will yield a reliable sample of all behaviors. This process is descriptive, not evaluative in nature and is designed to give the teacher a "handle" on the complex reality of the classroom, and provide a means of interpreting actions.

The\V.T.R. system was felt to be an important addition to the project because of the advantages of immediate playback for both the teacher and for other members of the social studies department. It also could provide a means of overcoming schedule conflict for peer group observations. The peer group (the social studies department) was selected as the basic unit for this project for several reasons: common interest and objectives in teaching; past experience in working together as a team; and the assumption that the individuals' act of assessing others in the teaching process would be constructive to that individual's own teaching.

HARDWARE

1. 7 Television UHF-VHF Monocrome Receivers
2. 7 Wall brackets for sets
3. 20 Memorax video tapes
4. 1 Zoom lens
5. 1 5000 Ampex tape recorder
6. 1 David Sanford dolly tripod
7. 1 EV 3647 mike-adaptor
8. 1 Dynair Mini-mod modulator
9. 1 Motorola monitor
10. 1 Heavy-duty cart

Note: (1) the Kettering Project provided part of the total needed, with the New York Mills Board of Education paying the rest, (2) the teacher improvement project was only one part of the total planned utilization and used only part of total equipment provided.

PLANNED PROCEDURE

The project on teacher improvement at New York Mills was late in starting and consequently will not be initiated until sometime after the 1968-69 action year.

The social studies department, during the spring semester of 1969 began the process of learning the Flanders Interaction Analysis system using materials provided by the Kettering Project for this purpose and the manual, *Interaction Analysis in the Classroom: A Manual for Observers* by Ned A. Flanders. It has been estimated that the time necessary to learn the skills of the system and build up group inter-reliability takes about ten hours. The group, at the same time, began to experiment with the use of the V.T.R. as a means of teacher improvement.

Early next semester the group met to discuss with representatives of the Kettering Project the philosophy, methods, and techniques of the Flanders system of observation. At this time the group planned peer group observations of teachers using this system of classifying teacher-student behavior, videotaping where possible, and time periods for the group or members of the group to meet for assessing and interpreting these observations and videotapes.

SCIENCE

Innovation 7: Test the effectiveness of Harvard Project physics as a substitute for the traditional high school physics.

Teacher: Mr. Louis Cizza   Grade: Eleventh and Twelfth
School: Utica Free Academy   Length of Program: One Year

RATIONALE FOR INNOVATION

1. To compare the results of Project Physics with the traditional approach.
2. To encourage more student participation in the instructional process.
3. To utilize the new technologies now available to education.

HARDWARE

Many of the materials and equipment that were designed for use with the Project Physics were purchased. This included laboratory apparatus, 8mm loop films, projectors, cameras to name a few.

CURRICULUM MATERIALS

Special materials were produced for Project Physics. Teachers' guides, student guides, and physics readers were purchased.

CLASSROOM ACTIVITIES

1. Students were able to work at their own pace in conducting laboratory experiments.
2. Extensive use was made of demonstrations.
3. Media of various kinds were used as part of the instructional process.
4. The discovery method was used quite effectively.
5. The inquiry method was used extensively with good result.

OBSERVED DIFFUSION

1. Other science teachers in the building were interested in the approach used.
2. Other physics teachers in the region want to introduce Project Physics into their curriculum.

Innovation 8: Utilization of a portable closed circuit television system for science instruction and in-service training.

Teacher: Mr. Ronald Kodra   Grade:
School: Mt. Upton Central School   Length of Program: One Year

RATIONALE FOR INNOVATION

1. Facilitate curriculum development
2. Promote cultural features

3. To aid in the assessment of teaching
4. Provide field trip summaries and introductions
5. To videotape unusual or difficult laboratory experiments.

HARDWARE

1. The Portable SONY Closed Circuit Television System 2200 Series including:
   a. video camera
   b. video recorder
   c. television receiver (monitor)
   d. necessary cables and connectors
   e. tripod
   f. additional omni-directional microphones (on loan)

CURRICULUM MATERIALS

While it was anticipated that videotapes would be produced for a variety of classroom activities, such was not the case.

— classrooms did not lend themselves to the operation of the video systems (only one electrical outlet available in some cases)

— time to produce such tapes proved to be a scarce commodity

Utilization of the video system: Perhaps one of the more extensive uses of the portable video system involved the training of the four faculty members in Flanders Interaction Analysis. As part of this Kettering Project sponsored program, each teacher was videotaped during a regular classroom session. These tapes provided the material for subsequent group analysis. The program extended over a seven-week period. This group of teachers developed skills in utilizing Flanders observational techniques for analyzing teacher-student verbal behavior.

CLASSROOM ACTIVITIES

Some science demonstrations were videotaped for class presentations, but classroom difficulties limited effectiveness: electrical outlets, limited laboratory and lecture space.

OBSERVED DIFFUSION

The elementary school principal experimented with the television system by videotaping his teachers and later discussing the topic with the individual.

Innovation 9: Utilization of a portable closed circuit television unit in a junior high science course.

Teacher: Mr. Donald Howard   Grade: Seventh — Ninth
School: Edmeston High School   Length of Program: One Semester

RATIONALE FOR INNOVATION

1. To videotape selected science classes for later viewing.
2. To develop a series of videotapes on selected topics.
3. To videotape field trips.
4. To videotape lengthy or difficult laboratory experiments for later viewing.
5. To overcome the problems involved in keeping students after school for make-up work. (Videotapes would allow students time during the school day to view missed material.)

HARDWARE

The portable Closed Circuit Television System 2100 Series:

a. Camera
b. Videcorder
c. 21 inch monitor
d. All necessary cables and connectors
e. Battery operated portable system
f. Battery charger

CLASSROOM ACTIVITIES

1. The instructor attempted and was successful in videotaping several field trips with the battery pack television system. On one occasion, he videotaped the stocking of the local trout stream for later viewing and discussion in the classroom.

2. Several science laboratory demonstrations were taped for future use. The construction of an ellipse proved particularly worthwhile.

3. Student presentations of laboratory experiments were taped for evaluation and analysis.

OBSERVED DIFFUSION

1. The English department used the ITV for speech and drama presentations.

2. The athletic department explored uses on ITV for baseball and track events. The videotape provided feedback for the players.

3. The music department investigated the possibility of using the equipment for the playback or marching drills and band rehearsals. Individual band members could be singled out for correction or praise.

4. The chemistry teacher attempted to videotape laboratory demonstrations.

5. The faculty taped their stage presentation of "Harvey".

6. As Mr. Howard introduced ITV into his classroom, those teachers in classrooms around him, who in this case were all English teachers, investigated and experimented with the system.

7. The equipment was demonstrated in the faculty lounge by the Kettering staff for one day.

8. Mr. Howard, himself, demonstrated to individual teachers how to operate the equipment.

9. Two junior high school students learned the operation of the equipment.

TEACHER EVALUATION

1. The instructor felt that too much of a production was made of the demonstrations he videotaped. Several periods were spent on preparation in some cases and the question is now raised whether or not it was worth the time and effort expended.

2. He raised the fundamental question of whether or not a student would retain the information longer when presented on videotape than when presented with traditional methods. The question of "value" of the videotape presentations was raised.

3. Consideration for special study carrels must be raised to eliminate the tendency for students viewing videotapes in the science class to bother one another.

4. More time is certainly needed for the instructor to develop ideas for the full implementation of the equipment.

5. Mr. Howard raised the question of splicing videotape to present tapes without serious flaws. He saw the need of having a physical splicing device. (These are readily available.)

6. Mr. Howard expressed the thought that teachers need to be given more freedom to implement their own innovations.

Innovation 10:   A comparison of the experimental Earth Science Curriculum Project (ESCP) with a standard Earth Science program.

Teacher: Mr. Anthony Militello   Grade: Ninth – Twelfth
School: Utica Free Academy   Length of Program: One Year

RATIONALE FOR INNOVATION

1. To compare the effectiveness of the lab-oriented ESCP with the traditional earth science course.
2. To discuss the innovative procedures with regional earth science teachers at monthly conferences.
3. To evaluate the results at the close of the school year and compare the progress of the experimental class with the control group.

HARDWARE

In addition to standard charts, globes and mineral specimens available at UFA, the Kettering Project supplied a complete set (for 30 students) of the approved laboratory equipment for the experimental class.

CURRICULUM MATERIALS

Copies of *Investigating the Earth* the official textbook, and lab manuals were issued to each student in the experimental group. The control group used *The World We Live In* by Namowitz and Stone, both the text and lab manual. Maps and field guides were supplied by the New York State Education Department.

CLASSROOM ACTIVITIES

1. Teams were formed to investigate earth science problems of the local area, such as weathering, pollution, and effects of climate.
2. The "county fair" technique was used frequently as a method of investigating several problems during one laboratory period.
3. The work of the experimental group was oriented at least 80% to lab and discussion.

OBSERVED DIFFUSION

1. Earth science teachers in the Utica region were informed monthly of the progress of the ESCP activities.
2. General Science teachers at UFA were invited to observe the experimental group and as a result more of the earth science classes next year will use this experimental approach.

TEACHER EVALUATION

1. Although ESCP requires more preparation on the part of the teachers, it is more satisfying to teach the course in this manner.
2. The students become active participants and assume more responsibility in the lab and class.
3. Evaluation procedures are built-in as the course progresses.

Innovation 11: **Utilization of portable closed circuit television in a high school chemistry class.**

Teacher: Mr. James Welty   Grade: Eleventh and Twelfth
School: Oriskany Falls High School   Length of Program: One Year

RATIONALE FOR INNOVATION

1. To investigate the uses of closed circuit television as a possible solution to crowded conditions in chemistry laboratory.
2. To produce videotapes for students' viewing of laboratory experiments (analytical balance, titration, and others).
3. To videotape potentially dangerous experiments.
4. To experiment with different audio-visual formats on videotape.
5. To provide an alternative to remodeling classroom with laboratory units along the walls.
6. To allow the instructor more time to work with individual students.
7. To compare televised instruction with the usual instructional format.

8. To begin a videotape library.
9. To provide feedback to students for personal evaluation.

HARDWARE

The SONY Tri-Pak —

1. Camera
2. Lighting equipment
3. Videocorder
4. Texts on instructional television
5. Monitor
6. Journal articles
7. Necessary cables and connectors
8. Bibliography on ITV
9. 7 reels of videotape
10. Film loops on demonstrations
11. Earphones
12. Equipment catalogs

CURRICULUM MATERIALS

1. There was no apparent increase in utilization of materials from BOCES or any other curriculum center.
2. Attempts were made to integrate media (ITV) into chemistry curriculum. However, more work is needed here to demonstrate the full potential of any media let alone ITV.
3. As for the development of a video tape library, the instructor (Mr. Welty) now realizes the inherent difficulties involved with such a project. Time, money, production techniques, and subject matter analysis are a few of the factors needing further examination.

SUCCESSFUL CLASSROOM ACTIVITIES

1. Several different chemistry laboratory experiments were videotaped. These were later viewed by the students. Student evaluation of the taped materials suggests that locally produced videotapes are acceptable and feasible for instruction.
2. The television camera was used by the instructor to examine microscopic organisms. The entire class was able to view on the monitor the activity beneath the microscope. In this case, without any additional equipment, the television camera was affixed to the classroom microscope.
3. Student performance was videotaped and evaluated for selected class experiments (titration and the analytical balance). A criteria of acceptable performance was developed by the instructor for these experiments. The students were evaluated in terms of how accurately they followed procedures.
4. Video recordings were made of relevant science programs (space and ocean explorations) from commercial television.
5. The video equipment was used outside the chemistry classes, for example:
   a. A videotape was made using programming principles for the study of light refraction.
   b. Certain elementary school classes experimented with uses of videotape — reading, role-playing, show and tell, and observation of class activities.
   c. A videotape was made of "A Day at Oriskany Falls" shown at the P.T.A. Open House.
   d. The video equipment was used extensively in taping sports events, football, soccer, track.

e. The English department used videotape for speech evaluation.

f. The administration experimented with pre-recorded videotapes at teachers' meetings.

DIFFUSION OF INNOVATION

1. The use of ITV in Oriskany Falls High School began with Mr. James Welty in chemistry. It was then tried by a friend in the English department, later by a first-year teacher in reading, and now the social studies teacher is thinking about possible uses.

2. Several teachers used the equipment for the playback of prerecorded materials.

3. Diffusion of the innovation was facilitated by Mr. Welty's demonstration of the equipment in the teachers' room and at teachers' meetings.

4. Other teachers came to his room to observe the operation involved.

5. The equipment was demonstrated for parents at an open house.

6. Teachers from outside the school (Utica) visited to observe the uses of video equipment.

TEACHER EVALUATION

1. The television equipment performed without severe maintenance problems. One TV cable was replaced along with minor adjustments made on the monitor. Recording heads and other critical components functioned without difficulty for the school year.

2. Additional knowledge of the idiosyncracies of the equipment is necessary. For example, videotape can be ruined if proper procedures are not followed in moving from "play" to "rewind" on the videocorder.

3. The editing controls were a welcomed feature. This permitted adding sound and new visuals to a videotape.

4. To develop videotapes of better quality, the instructor realizes the problem ahead — developing a small studio with proper lighting, appropriate sound systems, additional video equipment and more training in production techniques.

5. More time is needed to exploit fuller use of equipment. The instructor spent his own time to develop the recorded material used for the course.

6. Administrative leadership in innovation is needed to provide the opportunities for the innovator to function. Encouragement, time off to experiment and other incentives are needed to provide a stimulus.

7. Because of New York State cutbacks in funds, the instructor in this project felt that money would not be made available for additional videotapes and television components next year.

8. More training is necessary for the innovator to establish the "new practice" in a school setting. This training should go beyond mere technical skills. More needs to be done in understanding the process of innovation as it pertains to education.

Innovation 12:   Project teaching in Advanced Biology

Teacher: Mrs. Madelene Snyder   Grade: Twelfth

School: Canastota Senior High School   Length of Program: One Year

RATIONALE FOR INNOVATION

Formerly in the Biology program students in the Advanced Biology class were "exposed" to the same areas simultaneously, using the traditional techniques:

1. background of the area

2. laboratory techniques in the area

3. research problem in the area

An "area" might be (1) cells, (2) life in the pond waters, (3) algae, etc.

In September 1969, the Advanced Biology class of Canastota Central School applied innovative techniques to the studies for the year. That is, the following approach was taken:

1. selection of a problem
2. investigation of this problem at an intensive level
3. research and investigation to be done at the individual level, or in groups of two
4. report to be written in the scientific method

The aims of the course as presented to the students in September were the aims of individual study:

1. a great opportunity for the student
2. a challenge for the student

In particular the challenges to the student were:

1. ability to select a problem
2. ability to address himself to the problem so that he would gain an insight and a keen understanding of the selected topic
3. ability to organize himself so that the demanding work of research could be fitted into a busy school schedule
4. to become very facile in the laboratory
5. to so understand the problem, and his results that he might even do original research

The requirements of the students for the course were as follows:

1. research a problem
2. write (state) the aims of the problem
3. design a 10th grade laboratory exercise, or as a 10th grade research project in the regular biology classes
4. prepare a slide-tape review of the research
5. oral presentation of research at a symposium
6. record all the data and observations in a notebook
7. record all readings on card file
8. make responses to Kettering requests
   a. questionnaire
   b. tests

HARDWARE

1. Photovolt
2. Colony counter
3. Tape recorder
4. Slide projector
5. Spider cages
6. Skinner box
7. Autoclave
8. Animal cages
9. Microtome
10. Population studies box
11. Chromatographic columns
12. Klett colorimeter
13. Incubators
14. Hand-made light box

CLASSROOM ACTIVITIES

Speakers:

To present the scientific method, three speakers were used during the first and second week of classes.

1. Sheila Tornatore — 1968 graduate with 3 years of research work on Drosophila
2. Carol Mackay — NIH research scientist (virus transmission)
3. Dr. Theodore Peters — research scientist at Mary Imogene Hospital at Cooperstown, New York
4. Mrs. Bosworth — Canastota School Psychologist

Field trips:

Class trips
1. Colgate University Library
2. Vernon-Verona-Sherrill Central School — to hear Dr. Goodwin on BATS
3. Cornell University — to visit several scientists
4. Cooperstown (Dr. Peters) — to visit research laboratory and electron microscope

Individual trips
1. Oneida laboratory
2. Morrisville Bacteriology Laboratory
3. Colgate Psychology Laboratory
4. Colgate Library
5. Hamilton College Psychology Laboratory
6. Colgate Research Laboratory
7. Cornell Research Scientists (2 trips)

Symposia:

Three of these were held throughout the year and each student presented a review of his research project. Slides of their work and transparencies as well as actual parts of their research were shown. Guests were invited including: students, teachers, administrators, Colgate-Kettering personnel, parents, interested individuals, and those giving any aid to the students.

Open House:

Parents, administrators, students and teachers were invited to this as well as the members of a 4th grade class. At this open house each student set up materials and equipment used in his project.

OBSERVED DIFFUSION

There was a great deal of osmosis and diffusion between the members of each team, as there should have been. Of real significance, was the real interest exhibited between the various individuals and teams. I believe that each of the 16 members acquired a good knowledge of all other project. In some instances, a valuable exchange of ideas occurred. In others, students readily helped each other when "things got rough".

Real, hard evidence of diffusion to members of the school was the entrance into the class well after the term had begun. Two new students entered, one 10 weeks late, and one at midterm, both of these because of the interest brought about by members of the class.

Many members of the 10th grade biology classes became regular visitors and helpers. Much interest was shown by many science students and all of the science faculty.

There is only a little evidence that the interest was carried over to other classes. I do know that the idea of individual studies was discussed in a few classes. Most of the members of the advanced biology class feel that individual studies has great merit. Mr. Evans, principal, was always interested in our projects and was of great help in planning trips or anything different we wanted to do.

TEACHER EVALUATION

I believe that there is much to be said for individual studies and it is difficult to make a true evaluation since I did not complete the year's study. However, I have kept abreast of each of the projects, attended the two symposia held after I left, and feel that I can honestly say that the students really enjoyed their work. I make an effort at holiday time when former students return to have them discuss with current members the merits of each course. I feel it would have been better to have had some formal time built into the course. Perhaps the course should be for only one half of a year, if it is to be based on individual studies. It might be that 10 weeks of the year could be devoted to techniques, where every student acquired the knowledge and practice to become familiar with certain basic techniques. I believe, if I were to teach such a course again, that I would use a period of introduction, rather formal, rather than starting individual projects immediately.

Innovation 13:   Biology honors program

Mr. Joseph Gee   Grade: Twelfth
School: Clinton Senior High School   Length of Program: One Year

RATIONALE FOR INNOVATION

The Biology Honors Program was instigated primarily as an outgrowth of the work done at Colgate University in the Cooperative College-School Science Program. The two previous summers were spent at Colgate working with a small group in a laboratory oriented program.

The Biology Honors in Clinton is of such a nature that there is no established curriculum to follow. In part the nucleus for the idea of the course arose from an article in the *American Biology Teacher** and Brandwein's book, *A Book of Methods.*

HARDWARE

The original six students were each working on a separate project in the program. The equipment necessary included the following:

1.	Animal Conditioning	1.	Skinner Box; Cages
2.	Plant Growth Experiments	2.	Plant Growth Chamber
3.	Blood Studies	3.	Constant Temp Bath; Microscope
4.	Insectivorous Plants	4.	Waring Blender
5.	Genetic Studies	5.	Incubator; Microscope
6.	Photomicrographic Studies	6.	Camera, Adapter lens; Dark Room Equipment

TEACHER EVALUATION

The tangible result of the biology honors program was that it is going to become a regularly scheduled class in our science department. Another result was the inception of a physics program aimed at the non-regents level.

There were two changes that we felt would be beneficial to the program here in Clinton. The first was that the students work in at least pairs on a project.

The work with Mormoniella instead of Drosophilia for genetic studies was made possible in part by the cooperation of the Carolina Biological Supplies Customer Service Section. They provided the only work we were able to find on Mormoniella. The most comprehensive set of ideas for projects came from the *B.S.C.S. Research Problems in Biology.* Their books come in sets of four and provide innumerable projects for the high school biology program.

Help was also found when ideas for construction of laboratory equipment was needed in Barrett's book on building of laboratory equipment. Ideas for the plant growth studies was obtained from Klein's book on *Discovering Plants.* The procedure for blood studies was obtained from Harrow's *Biochemistry Laboratory Manual.*

Innovation 14:   Use of videotape in a Biology Lab

Teacher: Mr. Francis A. DeGrenier   Grade: Tenth and Twelfth

School: Cazenovia Central School   Length of Program: One Year

RATIONALE FOR INNOVATION

Assuming that actual participation in a laboratory activity is the best way to teach a laboratory concept, what would be the best alternative should doing the laboratory exercise be impossible?

HARDWARE

1.   Videotape Recorder (VTR) Sony
2.   Camera
3.   Monitor

CLASSROOM ACTIVITIES

The VTR was used primarily in the biology laboratory, however, other teachers made use of the equipment for enrichment, e. g. videotapes of news or special interest broadcasts, guest speakers at local colleges, etc.

TEACHER EVALUATION

The VTR was most successful when we used it to magnify objects through the microscope or to enlarge small objects in demonstration lectures. It was least successful when used to videotape lectures.

It was felt that unless equipment is stationed in the room, teachers would stop using it once the novelty has worn off. (New or unusual use of the equipment should be passed on from teacher to teacher, perhaps by a newsletter.)

Time was a major problem. It was found that a simple 10-minute presentation might require hours of preparation.

Future plans point toward the development of a tape-library of laboratory procedures for student use.

Innovation 15:   An intensive study of the anatomy of the cat – an advanced
**   biology project**

Teacher: Mrs. Elinor Bellinger   Grade: Twelfth

School: Vernon-Verona-Sherrill   Length of Program: One Year

RATIONALE FOR INNOVATION

Innovation is good, however, I do not agree with innovation solely for the sake of innovation. Also an innovation at one grade level, area, or school system may work very well but not be of value in another situation.

At VVS our innovation in advanced biology came about as a result of the instructors becoming bored with teaching the same old thing in the same old way. The funds allocated by the Kettering Project became the impetus for evaluating, reorganizing and revising the course of study. As a result the lecture-recitation approach was revamped and became a student-centered lab approach.

HARDWARE

The Kettering monies were used primarily for purchase of equipment such as a Heath Impscope, oversize dissecting trays, quality dissecting equipment as well as reference books.

TEACHER EVALUATION

I think the best evaluation that could be made of the course can be taken from student evaluation paragraphs:

"Why haven't we been taught science this way before?"

"I found learning the muscles and bones much easier and more fun having to find them myself rather than having the teacher lecture about them."

"I still hate the cats and can't bear to touch them." — (only negative criticism)

"I like being given a unit of work with a time schedule and we work at our own pace."

"At first some people in our group did not do their share of the work but after failing a couple of quizzes they really worked."

"The one course in high school I will never forget. It was wonderful."

As the instructor I believe I enjoyed the course as much as the students, the only complaint being that I wish I could have spent more time in developing some labs. I believe a couple (circulation especially) were too long; some directions too detailed or confusing. These areas are marked for future changes.

MATHEMATICS

Innovation 16:   **Application of an Electronic Calculator to a Mathematics Curriculum**

Teacher: Mrs. Virginia Reina   Grade: Eleventh and Twelfth
School: Frankfort-Schuyler Central School   Program Length: One Semester

RATIONALE FOR INNOVATION

In order to keep pace with modern technology, we should begin to instruct the students in the type of thinking involved in programming computers and the theory involved in the operation of computers. This exposure to computers was started several years ago with an NDEA grant for some basic training devices. The teacher then examined several types of electronic calculators and this project funded the machine that was finally selected. Since that time two NDEA grants have added more equipment so that class now has access to an additional calculator and a powerful computer. The students are now exposed to computer technology that is integrated into the school curriculum.

HARDWARE

1. Logic trainer
2. Monroe Epic 300 Electronic Printing Calculator
3. Wang Electronic Calculator with 4 keyboards
4. Teletypewriter connected to a time-sharing computer

CURRICULUM MATERIALS

1. Overhead transparencies prepared by teacher
2. Equipment manuals and workbooks
3. Books and pamphlets on computers

CLASSROOM ACTIVITIES

1. The overhead projector was used to help instruct the students in computer programming.
2. Students would put their programs on transparencies and the class would react to them.
3. During the class period the students had access to the machine.

OBSERVED DIFFUSION

1. Business Education Department used the machine in its classes.
2. Chemistry and physics instructors used the machine in their curricula.
3. Several teachers used the machine for calculations of various kinds.

4. The machine was demonstrated for the P.T.A., Science Fair, American Education Week, and County Mathematics meeting.
5. Teachers from other school systems visited the project.
6. Several articles appeared in the local paper describing the project.

TEACHER EVALUATION

1. The machine was very trouble free.
2. It was very simple to operate the machine.
3. It took only a few days to teach the students how to operate the machine.
4. Students were very enthusiastic about using the machine.
5. For the first time in many years students have shown an extra interest in math.
6. This was one of the most enjoyable years I have taught.
7. Students need time on the machine so the machine must be readily available.
8. It was difficult to cover all the material because of time limitations.

Innovation 17:   Application of an Electronic Calculator to a Mathematics Curriculum

Teacher: Mr. William Teeter   Grade: Eleventh
School: Ilion High School   Length of Program: Ten Weeks

RATIONALE FOR INNOVATION

1. Improve instruction
2. Increase student motivation
3. Individualize instruction

HARDWARE

Wang 320 Electronic Calculator with one keyboard and a CP-1 card programmer.

CURRICULUM MATERIALS

1. Overhead transparencies prepared by the teacher
2. Handouts prepared by the teacher
3. Equipment manuals and workbooks

CLASSROOM ACTIVITIES

1. The overhead projector was used to teach functions of the machine.
2. When not used in class, the machine was available in a seminar room so individual students could use it.
3. The machine was used as a device to demonstrate mathematical concepts to the class. A small podium was designed so students could view the readout.
4. As functions of the machine were needed in the curriculum they were introduced to the class.

OBSERVED DIFFUSION

1. Other math and science teachers used the machine on occasion.
2. The machine was demonstrated at a P.T.A. meeting, faculty meeting, and open house for American Education Week.
3. A demonstration was given to several teachers from another school.

TEACHER EVALUATION

1. The calculator was very dependable and easy to operate.
2. Equipment could be moved on a small cart which allowed it to be used in more than one location.
3. Students grasped the operation of the machine quickly.
4. Having enough extra class time to work with the machine is a problem.
5. The calculator lends itself well to the higher level math courses.

Innovation 18:   Uses of the computer in classroom testing

Teacher: Ernest Stockwell   Grade: Eleventh and Twelfth
School: Rome Free Academy   Length of Program: Eleven Months

RATIONALE FOR INNOVATION

The fundamental premise of this experiment was that the computer could be a very valuable tool in the improvement of classroom testing and, consequently, classroom instruction. The way in which this could be accomplished as well as the advantages and disadvantages of this application of the computer were to be explored. More specifically, the following objectives were sought:

1. The development of more objective evaluation techniques.
2. Increase the uniformity of evaluation among teachers.
3. Insure more uniformity in the content of basic course of study, through more uniform test construction.
4. Develop, over a period of time, a reliable instrument for the evaluation of achievement in a given course of study.
5. Improve classroom tests using item analysis.
6. Establish school norms for achievement. These might be norms other than the 70% passing grade.
7. Improve final examinations by making item analysis feasible.
8. Improve the grading of final examinations by making it possible to determine poor or unfair questions immediately and therefore not penalize the student.
9. Define more precisely areas of weakness in instruction or achievement after each unit and reinforce them at once.

Since it was desired to test instructional units and to follow through with a final examination at the end of the year, the classes in Intermediate Algebra were officially chosen for this experiment. The course Elementary Analysis was also used. Intermediate Algebra is an eleventh-year course and Elementary Analysis a twelfth-year course. Courses in which Regents Examinations are offered were excluded because it would not be feasible to follow through with final examinations scored on the computer. It is expected that there will be some use of the computer in evaluation in these courses in the future. The experiment was under the direction of the Department Chairman with four classroom teachers doing the bulk of the work.

HARDWARE

The equipment available for this experiment was an IBM 360/30 computer with disc drives, a card read/punch machine and a printer. The test scoring computer program was supplied by IBM.

CLASSROOM ACTIVITIES

The same unit tests were used by all teachers. While this had some initial disadvantage through passing of information between classes, it was not a serious problem after students learned that by passing information they only lowered their own grades. Unit tests for all classes were scored at the same time so that all students would be measured together. All teachers participated in the preparation of each test. Through the item analysis provided by the computer, teachers were able to determine poor questions and write better questions as the year progressed. In the discussion which accompanied the preparation of tests, teachers reached a greater accord on what was to be emphasized and what was to be included or excluded in a particular unit. Course modification and improvement were and will be a continuing by-product.

OBSERVED DIFFUSION

It was hoped that the use of the computer for test scoring and analysis of classroom instruction would be generated beyond this experiment. This happened to a degree beyond expectation. Another very valuable project in mathematics was started in the junior high schools and three other departments, social studies, biology and driver education have made extensive use of the facility. The English Department is considering it for next year.

Achievement and uniformity of instruction and evaluation have been a frustrating problem with one particular ability group in the seventh and eighth grades. In an effort to find a new approach to this problem, teachers in the seventh grade were asked to help prepare "progress tests" which would be scored and analyzed on the computer. The tests would be given to all students in this group in both junior high schools. There would be two such tests, one each at the end of the second and fourth marking periods. (There are six marking periods in the school year.) Their tests were practice for the final examination which was machine scored and analyzed. The progress tests were not used for grading purposes unless the teacher wished to do so. In fact, they were administered after marks for the period were turned in. This project turned out to be so successful that next year the teachers have requested that more frequent meetings be held to establish more precise guidelines on what is to be a minimum course of study, to conduct progress tests after each marking period except the last one which will be followed by the final examination. An effort will be made to establish a testing instrument which can be used to determine the success or failure of a student to achieve the minimum competency for credit in seventh grade mathematics. It is also planned to extend the project into the eighth grade.

Several biology teachers have used the computer for unit testing through the year with excellent results. It cannot be used for scoring of the Biology Regents examination yet, but this is a goal of this particular department.

Several social studies teachers have also taken advantage of this facility throughout the year. Final examinations in Non-Regents World History, Non-Regents American History and Part I of Regents World History were scored on the computer. The success of this operation varied according to whether or not the teacher has used the service during the year and whether or not the students had had experience with the materials (answer card and pencil). The importance of prior practice and experience with this type of test scoring to success with final examinations was evident.

The Driver Education Department has used the service in two ways. They have used it for scoring final examinations and for the development of an attitude survey. They are attempting to identify attitudes which indicate good and poor drivers.

The Statistics classes have also made use of the computer to evaluate an opinion survey. Their final examination was scored on the computer.

EVALUATION

The following evaluation of this experiment is a reflection of the experience and opinions of the teachers and the department chairman as a result of one year's work.

The construction of objective test items was more difficult and time consuming than had been anticipated. Some teachers found it more difficult than others. Teachers greeted the task with varying degrees of enthusiasm. Nevertheless, it was definitely demonstrated that with sufficient imagination and motivation teachers can prepare objective (multiple choice) questions which measure achievement in nearly every area of mathematics instruction in Intermediate Algebra and Elementary Analysis. As experience and practice were gained teachers were able to prepare better questions with less effort. Measurement of the understanding of mathematical concepts and skills is possible. Questions testing rote memorization and simple recall were minimal.

Since each unit was tested only once and only one final examination was prepared, it can hardly be said that the most effective instruments for measuring achievement were arrived at. This will never be the case since emphasis and content will change. The final examination was a reflection of the best items of measurement in the unit tests. As a result, it was a better reflection of achievement than were the unit tests. It was rewarding to have the teachers willing, some desirous, of continuing the program another year in spite of the additional work which it entailed. It is not expected that as much time will be needed in another year because the experience of this year will make test item preparation easier and there is a good bank of test items from which to draw. All prepared questions, used and unused, have been saved.

While the ultimate success with computer scoring of classroom tests is still a long way off, it can be said that a significant start has been made. The enthusiasm which has been generated is certain to spread. The benefits to the students in instruction and achievement may be difficult to measure objectively, but they are clearly evident.

It is interesting to note that a total of 1807 final examination papers, or parts thereof, were scored on the computer at the end of the year. While this may have saved time and work on the part of the teachers, the real benefit will come from the information provided about the test itself. If this aspect of the scoring and analysis is ignored, then it is doubtful that the expense and effort of making such scoring possible can be justified.

Innovation 19: Mathematical Curriculum Center

Teacher: Mrs. Leola S. Fassett   Grade: Eighth
School: Springfield Central School   Length of Program: Sixteen weeks

RATIONALE FOR INNOVATION

1. Increase understandings in mathematics by using new techniques.
2. Individualize instruction through the use of various media.
3. Provide enrichment and remedial materials for the students use.
4. Create more interest in mathematics by employing new methods and materials.

HARDWARE

1. Overhead projector
2. Cassette tape recorders
3. Super 8mm loop projector
4. Thermocopy machine

CURRICULUM MATERIALS

1. Mathematics games
2. Filmstrips
3. Teacher-made transparencies
4. Cassette tapes
5. Programmed slide rule sets
6. Transparency originals
7. Super 8mm loop films
8. Programmed materials
9. Books and pamphlets
10. Mathematics model kits
11. Transparency preparation materials

CLASSROOM ACTIVITIES

1. The overhead projector was employed extensively for classroom instruction.
2. The students played math games during free periods.

3. Independent study was used where possible.
4. Students used the new equipment and materials for class reports and demonstrations.

OBSERVED DIFFUSION
1. Worked closely with a teacher in a nearby school on curriculum development.
2. Teachers in the school interested in the innovation.
3. Demonstrations were given to the faculty.
4. A presentation was given to the school board.
5. An article was written for the school newspaper on the innovation.

TEACHER EVALUATION
1. The students enjoyed using the new equipment and materials.
2. Need better organization in order to find all the curriculum materials.
3. Had difficulty finding the time to cover the material in an innovative manner.
4. Need more time to work on curriculum development.
5. The school was very cooperative.

Innovation 20:   Mathematics Resource Center

Teacher: Mrs. Susan B. Culbert   Grade: Eighth
School: Owen D. Young Central School   Length of Program: Twelve Weeks

RATIONALE FOR INNOVATION
1. Enrich the mathematics curriculum with new materials.
2. Individualize instruction using new techniques.
3. Motivate student interest in mathematics.
4. Help students who need remedial work.

HARDWARE
1. Overhead projector
2. Cassette tape recorders

CURRICULUM MATERIALS
1. Mathematics games
2. Custom-made transparencies
3. Mathematics model construction kits
4. Math drill records
5. Cassette tapes
6. Slide rule sets
7. Pamphlets and books
8. Programmed materials
9. Transparency preparation materials
10. Transparency originals
11. Remedial and diagnostic materials

CLASSROOM ACTIVITIES
1. Used overhead transparencies a great deal for class instruction.
2. Used drill cassette tapes for remedial and diagonostic purposes.
3. Mathematics games and experiments were available during free time.
4. Individual students could use the various materials available for enrichment or remedial purposes.

OBSERVED DIFFUSION
1. Worked closely with a teacher in a nearby school on curriculum development.
2. One teacher sat in on a class for several weeks to learn new techniques.
3. Several teachers in the school used the new materials and techniques.

TEACHER EVALUATION
1. Students enjoyed many of the new materials and techniques.

2. It is important to have a system of organizing the materials so you can find them when you need them.
3. It was hard to find the time to do all the things I wanted to do.

Innovation 21:   Junior High Mathematics Laboratory

Teacher: Mr. Wayne Cook   Grade: Seventh
School: Greene Central School   Length of Program: Ten Months

RATIONALE FOR INNOVATION

Our current program in junior high mathematics, while presenting a modern approach to the subject, is failing to maintain the high level of interest and achievement which has been established in the elementary grades. One of the major factors which causes this decline is, I believe, the fact that we are forcing the pupils away from a free and direct contact with their subject. We are regimenting both bodies and minds into a staid, traditional pattern of seating and subject. I think that we could improve the performance and the attitudes of our math students by instituting a mathematics laboratory at the junior high level.

While the term laboratory usually denotes a place devoted to experimental study in one of the sciences, it can also connote any place where a subject is taught through a laboratory approach. In mathematics especially, this means a room where students are exposed to math through individual investigation and through experimentation by both individuals and groups. Students are encouraged to discover mathematical facts and concepts through the manipulation of objects, the design and construction of models, the serious inquiry and testing of hypotheses, the application of theory, as well as through reading and discussion. Through the imaginative and tactile approach which would be used in such a laboratory, the students would gain insight and understanding while retaining their essential interest and creativity.

HARDWARE

1.   Minivac 601 Computer Trainer
2.   Cassette Tape Recorder

CURRICULUM MATERIALS

1.   Mathematical Games
     A.   Tuff
     B.   Configurations
     C.   Equations
     D.   On Sets
     E.   Wff 'n Proff
     F.   Psycepaths
     G.   Tac-Tickle
     H.   Real Numbers Game
2.   Other Materials
     A.   Space spiders (3D curve)
     B.   SRA Computational Skills Kit
     C.   Mathematics Skill Builder
     D.   Understanding Mathematical Concepts (records & worksheets)
     E.   Pamphlets and books of a remedial or enrichment nature
     F.   Mathematical Originals for overhead projector
     G.   Math models
     H.   Sage Kit
     I.   Experiments in Mathematics

CLASSROOM ACTIVITIES

1. Give students a voice in what to study and/or how they wanted to work on it.
2. Whenever possible, an attempt to individualize study was made by using a large number of materials and methods.
3. Use methods for introducing daily lessons.
4. Small group activities such as: games, experiments, model building, etc.
5. Equipment and materials were available during free periods and after school for remedial work and enrichment.

OBSERVED DIFFUSION

The innovator, Mr. Cook, worked closely with a teacher in another subject area who was also an innovator for the project. Many other teachers showed interest in what the teachers were doing.

TEACHER EVALUATION

1. The teacher felt that the project as a whole was successful. Some methods and materials worked better than others so that constant revision was necessary. The project will be continued next year with some revisions.
2. By the end of the year the experimental group had a better attitude and performed somewhat better on examinations.
3. Most of the materials could be purchased by a school if budgeted over a period of several years.
4. With proper planning most of the materials fit into the curriculum.
5. Because of the experience acquired in selection materials, a better job can be done in future selections.
6. The students in the experimental group had more interest and enthusiasm in working with these various materials, than in traditional classroom methods and materials.

GENERAL*

Innovation 22:   Utilization of portable closed circuit television to supplement the administrator/teacher conference in the evaluation of teaching

Teacher: Mr. Lawrence Paser   Grade: Twelfth
School: Oxford Academy & Central School   Length of Program: One Year

RATIONALE FOR INNOVATION

1. To improve teaching through careful use of closed circuit television for self-evaluation.
2. To develop with the faculty a criteria for assessing teaching.
3. To videotape teacher-student classroom interaction.
4. To develop an acceptance of instructional television among the faculty, board, and parents.
5. To provide videotaped material for teacher/administration conferences.
6. To develop an acceptance of the need to study the teaching-learning process, and investigate observational systems, Flanders, etc.
7. Audiotape recorders had been used in the past to analyze instruction, but not being able to see the classroom interaction limited the usefulness of this approach.

HARDWARE

1. Kettering Project supplied the basic Sony 2200 series portable closed circuit television system.
   Camera and tripod
   7 reels of tape

*Innovations 4, 8, 9, 11, and 18 have general aspects in addition to departmental

Monitor – 23 inch
A small 11 inch monitor
Videocorder
An additional camera lens
Necessary cables and connectors

2. Concerning the operation and maintenance of the equipment, Mr. Paser made the following observations:
   1. All components functioned perfectly during the year.
   2. No recording or viewing time was lost due to malfunctioning equipment.
   3. A second camera, a camera switching mechanism, and additional sound equipment is needed to expand usage of the present system.
   4. Attempting to record student-teacher interaction continued to be a problem. Perhaps a microphone amplifier would eliminate this problem.
   5. The portable system has its limitations. On occasions teachers wanted a slow motion and stop action control. This can be done manually, but picture loss is extensive.
   6. Rather than moving the television equipment from classroom to classroom, a future consideration is to have one room set up permanently and to have classes move.

CURRICULUM MATERIALS

The thrust of this innovation centered on technology and teaching. Materials, as such, were not investigated outside the fact that in viewing the videotapes teachers were made aware of the need and potential for additional instructional materials whether in print or visual. One outcome of the awareness, of course, would be a surge in the use of BOCES materials.

SUCCESSFUL ACTIVITIES AND FUTURE PLANS FOR ITV

1. All teachers volunteering for the project were videotaped at two different times during the year. On each occasion an entire classroom period was recorded for later viewing. Attempts were made to record both teaching and student verbal interaction, but this was not always possible. In most cases, the equipment was set up to tape the teacher, and frequently, taping student responses and classroom behavior was possible.
2. Next year, the science department is planning to make use of the ITV system along the lines already developed in some other Kettering Projects. Videotaping laboratory experiments, enlarging microscope analysis, and developing a videotape library are under consideration.
3. Another consideration for ITV in the future is the availability of videotapes for make-up work for students. While this would involve a considerable amount of videotape, it does represent one solution for students out of school for extensive periods of time.
4. Beginning teachers in the district will have the first opportunity to utilize the ITV system for self-evaluation in the comming years.
5. Plans for developing a series of videotapes on relevant instructional process for viewing and discussion for beginning teachers are being developed.

OBSERVED DIFFUSION OF INNOVATION

1. Before the television system was used in any classroom, it was set up in the gymnasium for several weeks during lunch hour for students and teachers to become familiar with its operation.
2. The athletic department found quick use of the equipment for playback of various sporting events.

3. The English department utilized the equipment with recording a student drama.
4. One school board meeting was videotaped on an experimental basis for their own use.
5. During an open house the parents were made aware of the ITV system and its potential.

EVALUATION

1. One problem which prevented earlier involvement with the project in the school was the lack of enough videotape to record the teachers in the classrooms. As it was, the initial seven reels of tape were not enough. Consequently, it was not until late Fall that the school received enough additional tape to begin the task of videotaping the teachers in the project.
2. Finding the time to videotape all the teachers became a problem for the administrator who initially operated the equipment. Later in the school year, he received help from his media coordinator. Perhaps on another occasion the teachers themselves could do the videotaping.
3. The need for better sound systems became apparent, particularly when teacher-student verbal interaction was desired.
4. It was felt important in this type of project to have the support of the faculty.

EXPERIMENTAL DESIGN

It was planned initially to measure in some way the effect of instructional television in this school situation when used as an adjunct to the teacher-administrator conference. Mr. Paser proposed that one group (6 – 8 teachers) would observe themselves on videotape in conjunction with the usual teacher observation conference in the interest of improving their teaching abilities and skills. A second group for comparison would receive the usual observation conferences without videotape feedback although they were videotaped.

In Mr. Paser's judgment the videotape feedback supplied to the experimental group convinced him of the efficiency of such an undertaking. Unfortunately, other measures beyond personal judgment were lacking. An attempt was made, however, to develop as a working model a list of teaching behaviors deemed acceptable and relevant to that school and community. The faculty did develop a criteria for assessing their teaching. Unfortunately, however, in viewing a videotape, they discovered that factors other than those listed need to be taken into consideration. A system such as Flanders Interaction Analysis might provide the objectivity needed.

ENGLISH

Innovation 23:   Propaganda and the Video Tape in the Speech Class

Teacher: Mrs. Perreta (Department Chairman)   Grade: Eleventh
            and Mr. Tosti
School: Canastota Jr. – Sr. High School   Length of Program:
A Videotape recorder is being used in the study of propaganda in one class. It is also being used in a speech class. Guests are videotaped and the tape played in several classes. Students are creating tapes.

Innovation 24:   A Modified Humanities Course for the Non-college Bound

Teacher: Mrs. Ruth Yule   Grade: Twelfth
School: Cooperstown Central School   Length of Program:
A modified Humanities course for the non-college bound student using a student-centered and multimedia approach to learning.

Innovation 25:   A Composition Approach Using Cassettes

Teacher: Mr. Gary Rider   Grade: Twelfth

School: Hamilton Jr. – Sr. High School   Length of Program:

Composition was approached through the use of tape recorders. Each student had a cassette-type tape recorder. Some students recorded their research for later use, some dictated compositions, then corrected them on the tape before writing them out, some conducted interviews and many students used the equipment in all these ways and others. The teacher commented on the students' work on his own tape. The recorders were used in oral composition work and public speaking also.

Innovation 26:   Multi-Media for Creative Communication

Teacher: Mr. Jean Benoit   Grade: Ninth and Tenth

School: Madison Central School   Length of Program:

The project was a large step in the direction of a multi-media center for communications – (written and oral). Mr. Benoit hoped to develop creativity and improve expression of ideas and materials through the use of media. He hoped students might be able to improve in composition and speech work if they were able to see and hear themselves and their material. He hoped for much more concise expression and narrowing of topic into a more disciplined piece of work.

Innovation 27:   Laboratory for Reading

Teacher: Mrs. Ruth Denny   Grade: Seventh through Nineth

School: Milford Central School   Length of Program:

Team students with an older "buddy" for help in reading assignments. Team students with younger children and have them help teach these children to read better. Students listen to tapes of assignments being read by a good reader and following in the text. A tape standing (math, science, social studies).

Innovation 28:   Using the VTR as a Resource in Speech and Discussion Sessions

Teachers: Mrs. Alice Neill & Mrs. Abbie Jean Cooke   Grade: Eleven

School: Norwich Senior High School   Length of Program:

Mrs. Neill – The use of VTR in teaching English as a device to bring otherwise unattainable material to the students as well as taping students in speech and discussion sessions. Individual students did projects using the equipment also.

Innovation 29:   Self-Improvement through Use of Videotapes (9-12)

Teacher: Mrs. Rosemary Courtney   Grade: 9 – 12

School: Oneida Senior High School   Length of Program:

The senior speech students videotaped each others' speeches and then the class evaluated the content and speaking skill as well as posture, gestures and facial expressions. The students criticized each other in a constructive way and each person was able to "see himself as others saw him." Very often the students were more critical of themselves and each other than the teacher had been. Some network programs of speeches were used and some tapes were exchanged with other schools.

Innovation 30:   Writing Clinic Using Tape Recorders

Teacher: Mr. Joseph Martinelli   Grade: Tenth

School: Sherburne-Earlville Central High School   Length of Program:

Writing clinic using tape recorders. In a ten-day plan, three periods are devoted to "precision," the preparation for writing assignment. Two or three days are devoted to working with idea sheets, outlines, and final drafts. Compositions are corrected by the use of cassette tapes, not all at the same time. Some students are grouped according to their progress. Groups and individuals are assigned activities to suit their needs as evidenced in testing and actual performance.

Innovation 31:   Creativity in English for Non-Regents Seniors

Teacher: Mr. David Babcock   Grade: 12

School: Vernon-Verona-Sherrill Central School   Length of Program:

An activity centered course for non-regents seniors. Emphasis was on using movies, making movies, games, making tapes (oral), magazines, paperbacks, and plays. Creativity is encouraged greatly in individual projects, especially in the film making.

IMPROVEMENT IN RESEARCH MODELS AND INSTRUMENTS

It is the obligation of a research study of this kind to pass on to others some of the experience gained and problems encountered so that research can be improved. Our research procedures that others may find useful can be classified in two types: (1) research designs and problems encountered with them, and (2) evaluation instruments and new dimensions.

Stratification of Schools

One of the problems to which the study addressed itself was stratification of the sample so that the analysis could proceed as though dealing with a homogeneous population of schools.* There were two possible ways of handling the problem: (1) through delimitation, by selecting similar schools; or (2) through suitable post-hoc control, either by stratification or by regression analysis. Bases for stratifying are usually variables that are thought to be related to the criteria, such as social-economic level, sex, grade level and others.

As aspects of the cooperating schools became increasingly familiar to the staff, it became apparent that any comparison between these institutions might have to take into account differences in their relative sizes and financial resources. At least two of the schools in urban areas had as many staff members in their one department as some schools located in more isolated areas of the region had on their entire staff; furthermore, several of the schools which were equivalent in size differed widely in the amount and quality of their physical resources. It seemed plausible to assume that to some extent the level of sophistication and the quality of attitude toward innovation would correlate positively with some combination of (1) school size and (2) funds available to the district. In an attempt to determine the effects of these two variables on comparisons between schools, it was decided to classify them into distinct levels, or strata. The rationale for such a decision was the belief that schools within strata would be more alike in at least these two aspects than would be the schools in different strata.

The use of stratification afterwards is an expediency, and is not proposed as a recommended procedure to follow. The desire to assist schools in the region influenced many of the decisions prior to this stage. The sample of schools even stratified, is still non-random. For a concise discussion of post-hoc stratification, see Dubois.**Readers interested in use of stratification to specify in advance the patterning of confounding among the sources of variation should examine the example of fractional factorial design in Buckmiller and Miller.***

The procedure followed in accomplishing the stratification is the same as that outlined in detail in the Wisconsin study, with the difference that the original investigators placed a greater emphasis on the use of image, rather than principal components, factor analysis. In their report they explained their preference by contrasting the efficiency of the former with that of the latter. It would appear on

---

*For a complete study showing this stratification procedure, write for an article by Robert J. Crowley, *Post-Hoc Stratification of Schools.* The Kettering-Colgate Project, Colgate University, Hamilton, May 1970.

**Philip Dubois, *An Introduction to Psychological Statistics,* New York: Harper and Row, 1965.

***Archie Buckmiller and Donald A. Miller, *Multivariate Procedures for Stratifying School Districts.* (USOE Project 5-8043-2-12-1.) Final Report. Madison, Wisconsin. Instructional Research Laboratory, 1967.

the basis of their remarks that a principal components analysis could serve in the event that a computer program to perform an image analysis were unavailable, as proved to be the case in this instance.

The classification of the schools into levels required three stages: that of (a) preparing the data, which included its collection from different sources, and the substitution of estimated values for schools with data missing; (b) performing the factor analysis and deriving the factor scores; and (c) determining the strata patterns on the basis of these scores, whereupon schools were assigned to strata that correspond to their individual patterns.

The thirty-seven control and experimental schools were classified into five strata on the basis of size and funds available. A simple analysis of variance procedure was then used to determine whether there were significant differences among strata means with respect to the six criteria. In other words, should the experiment have controlled the size and financial factors if it intended to eliminate the influences of these two variables?

Table D-1 shows that differences in the criteria, due to schools belonging to different strata, were not significant for any of the pre-survey criteria or for gain on the criteria. The strata, however, did differentiate between schools with respect to availability and usage on the post-survey.

The question arises as to whether a correction should have been made in the post-survey criteria data. No correction was made. Perhaps it should have been. However, because there were no significant differences with respect to gains on the criteria and because financial resources was one of the forces to be studied in later multiple correlations and regression analyses, the differences among schools due to the strata were not controlled or factored out. Nevertheless, the technique is important and may be essential for many studies and especially for those relying solely on the experimental-control type of design (Design II).

Table D-1 Effect of Stratification on the Differences Among
Schools on the Three Criteria

A. Attitude and Attitude Gains Criteria

Strata	Pre-Survey Means	Attitude Post-Survey Means	Means Gains
1	2.9	2.6	.17
2	3.0	3.0	.04
3	2.9	3.1	.14
4	2.9	2.8	.02
5	2.8	2.8	.06
	F = .55	$ = .85	F =.41

B. Availability

Strata	Pre-Survey Means	Post-Survey Means	Means Gain
1	34.6	39.0	4.4
2	32.2	35.0	2.9
3	33.1	36.1	3.0
4	27.6	31.3	3.7
5	28.4	29.8	1.4
	F = 1.4	F = 3.0	F = .40

C. Usage

Strata	Pre-Survey Means	Post-Survey Means	Means Gain
1	33.0	38.2	5.2
2	32.1	33.1	1.0
3	33.1	36.8	3.6
4	27.3	31.8	4.5
5	27.4	30.2	2.8
	$F = 1.4$	$F = 3.0$	$F = .40$

*Needed F for significance is 2.87 at the .05 level.

Models for Measurement of Change

As stated at the beginning of this report, the problem of educational reform has been a crucial one for a long time. In the last thirty years, and especially in the last decade, attention has been increasingly focused on how to measure change. The problem can be thought of as being divided into two parts: (1) definition of change, and (2) need for an appropriate and accurate statistical model for measuring it.

Some studies, such as that of Hilliker, define educational change (the criteria) as innovativeness in the school. He used raters, but could have used other means, to determine how innovative the schools were. In that study the determination of innovativeness involved a measurement at only one occasion or time. The raters knew the schools and rated them with respect to their innovativeness at that time. Those schools whom the raters found to be more innovative had presumably changed more than others.

A quite different way of measuring change was used in the present study. It measured school innovativeness at two different times, two years apart. This model might be thought of as measuring the rate of change. That it was rate of change and not just innovativeness would be more evident if instead of being measured at two times, pre- and post-survey, each school was monitored every two years over a ten-year period. Five ratings of innovativeness over a period of years would then be available. Rate of change could then be calculated. Longitudinal studies of this kind have an advantage over cross-sectional or "one-shot" studies, partly because they focus on change. For example, in a quite different field, knowledge of change in public support for the policies of the President of the United States is at least as important as knowing the present climate of support.

In the present study, change was defined as the amount of gain each school made over a two-year period, the difference between where it stood at post-survey time and where it stood at pre-test time. The design is similar in concept to asking whether over a period of two years of training an athlete learns to jump higher. If he jumps seven feet high after two years training, when before he jumped only five feet, we would say that in high jumping he has gained two feet. Similarly a school that was rated having very little innovation (30 points) available in 1968, but as having a considerable amount available (60 points) would be said to have made a gain of 30 points in innovativeness. The gain or change in innovativeness is calculated by subtracting the pre-survey standing of the school from its post-survey standing. This is a simple and straightforward process provided the instruments used to measure the criteria have perfect reliability. However, few if any measures are perfectly reliable. So the question arises as to whether the top schools in

147

innovativeness in the pre-survey were rated too high and the low schools too low. The error for the top schools is more likely to be on the up side and vice versa for the low schools. A correction of factor may be needed.

As Campbell and Stanley* say, "Errors of inference due to overlooking regression effects have been troublesome in education research." In some studies, the regression effect could be important for Design I, as well as for Design II, depending on whether stratification variables differentiated among the schools.

If correcting for regression provides a more accurate estimate as to which schools gain the most, free of the influence of whether they score low or high on the pre-survey, we would want to use it. We would not want gain to be an index of whether a school was below average in innovations at the start.

The amount of correction for regression needed is due to two influences: (1) error of measurement (unreliability of the measures); and (2) the degree of correlation between the pre- and the post-test. The first influence has been discussed. With respect to the second influence, it can be said that the lower the correlation, the greater the regression toward the mean. This is true from the very definition of the correlation coefficient.

However, the lack of correlation may not be due to error. It may be due to an actual re-alignment in the standing of the schools that has resulted from the intervention of the project or from other important forces being studied. One would not wish to remove the real change that had taken place. As a matter of fact, if there were a perfect correlation between the pre- and post-survey results ($r = 1.0$), there would be no change. No school would have benefited more from the project than any other school and study of the relation of school and community forces to differences in school gain could not have been made. Such a study would be pointless because no school would have changed its relative standing.

This degree of correction (called regression), as far as is known, has not been used in any previously published study of educational change. For other types of study, such as those predicting future grades from aptitutde test scores, a correction is a necessity. If the regression technique is not used, students with high I.Q. will be predicted to make grades much higher than they actually do, and thus will seem to be under-achievers, while those with low I.Q.'s will seem to be performing beyond expectations (predicted grade) and will be viewed as over-achievers. In fact, the apparent results would be due to the tendency of the highs and lows to regress toward the mean because of error in the first measure, aptitude. It is possible that a similar phenomenon occurs when measuring educational change. Schools rated "very high" on the pre-test, are more apt to be rated too high rather than too low. On the actual post-test, they may show an artifically lower score than expected. As in the aptitude example, the most innovative schools will seem to gain less than expected, while the least innovataive may make larger aritfical gains.

A different way of reducing the regression influence due to error is to use a procedure employed in physics. In that discipline, measurements are made more than once and averaged to determine the best estimated measurement. For example, the diameter of a rod at a given temperature would be the average of more than one measurement. Also, in the present study, more than one measurement was taken: two independent raters for each school interviewed two to four informants. Thus, each school's final standing on each of the criteria was an average of two or

*Donald T. Campbell and Julian C. Stanley *Experimental and Quasi-Experimental Designs for Research,* Rand-McNally & Co., Chicago, 1966. p. 11.

148

more measurements. This should reduce the regression effect due to error of measurement (the first influence previously discussed). It also would reduce systematic errors due to bias on the part of the raters or informants, to the degree that the ratings were really made independently of each other.

With these considerations in mind, this study used both statistical models as indexes of gain. First the simple definition of gain (Post-score minus Pre-score); and second, regressed gain (Post-score minus predicted score).

The main body of the text reports correlation coefficients with the first type of gain only. In Chapter 11, both are reported in a study of the relative importance of school and community forces in influencing school gains. It should be noted here that the regression problems are relevant only for assessment of gain, and not for studying the schools at one particular time, such as either pre- or post-survey time. The problem is discussed here so that other researchers can consider the matter further.

Chapter 12 shows that for availability, approximately the same forces appeared to be most important, whether one used the simple or regressed gains model. For usage, two of the five forces were different.

A Comparison of the Usefulness of the Interview Case-Study Design and the Correlational Research Design

This study has used four research designs: (1) correlational, Design I; (2) experimental control group, Design II; (3) multiple correlation and regression, Design III; and (4) the interview case-study, Design IV. What are their relative merits? Do they duplicate each other or does each make its own particular contribution? This section will emphasize the relative merits of the four approaches.

The interview case-study approach focused on two schools, School A (large gain in innovativeness) and School B (little gain). Differences in gain are shown in Table D-2. Designs I and III surveyed 26 schools which also varied in innovativeness. Design IV (case approach) found that administrative leadership and the nature of its source of power were major elements in distinguishing between the two schools. Designs I and III tended to agree. The multiple correlation approach found that administrative leadership was among the top influences for Availability and Usage in 26 schools. When schools A and B were separated from the larger sample for study, administrative leadership scores were found to be 4.6 and 3.7, respectively (Table D-3). All these designs agreed on the importance of administrative leadership. Design IV went on to clarify what kind of administrative leadership was important.

The study of the organizational climate of the schools was also a common concern of three of the different research approaches. The correlational approach, Designs I and III, found that trust, openness and adaptability were related to gains in Attitude. Design IV showed that the two schools differed significantly in creativeness, problem-solving and development, all important characteristics for innovation. The two approaches agreed that climate was important, but identified different attributes of climate. This may have been because different measures were used. They agreed that School A and School B did not differ with respect to trust (Table D-4). In this respect School A was not representative of other more innovative schools in the sample. Design IV did not include measures of openness and adaptability.

Designs I and III gathered data beyond the walls of the school to obtain an understanding of characteristics and attitudes of board members and parents. They

149

showed that School A operated in a more innovative-conscious community than did School B. School A board members had more favorable attitudes toward innovation (4.6 compared to 3.4) and were more favorable toward the idea of putting pressure on the administration to work actively to support innovation. Parents in School A's community tended to accept new practices more favorably (3.1) than was the case in School B's community (2.6) (See Table D-5.)

The multiple correlation approach confirmed the importance of community forces. Also, it pointed to the influence of the Kettering-Colgate Project as an independent influence.

Designs I and III (Table D-2) showed that the students in School A gained more in participation in innovative practices than did those in School B. The former gained 4.23 points, compared to practically no gain for students in School B. These comparisons are sufficient to illustrate the relative contribution of each type of design.

Conclusions

1. Design II, the experimental-control group design, was helpful in determining whether the 26 schools as a group made a significantly greater gain, as a result of the project. Its weaknesses were two in numbers. First, it could not study the question of what forces were influencing scored schools to gain more than others. It, therefore, suffered from being too general for a study in which many forces were worthy of analysis. Second, it assumed an almost impossible condition; namely, that the so-called "control schools" are really controllable.

2. Designs I and III had several advantages. They could sample a larger number of schools because survey instruments were self-administering. The survey technique made possible the use of a large sample, which in turn made possible the correlation and multiple correlation techniques. It, therefore, is more desirable for a regional study in which the number of participating schools is large. All the schools in a project want to be evaluated. Also, because of efficiency, these designs could study a wider range of influences, such as those of parents, board members and students. For the participants and staff, this would have been very time-consuming, if done by interview.

3. Design IV had other relative strengths and shortcomings. It provided a better "feel" for the two systems in action. Usually, however, it had to delimit its study to a few variables, publics or schools. For the sample of two schools and a limited number of forces, it proved quite effective. Finally, its main contribution was to an understanding of the dynamics of the situations as observed by an expert interviewer.

Results for Schools A and B, from Designs I, III and IV, tended to be in agreement with respect to Schools A and B. Although Design IV delimited its study to two schools and to two forces (administrative patterns and organizational climate) its findings in these respects were consistent with those based on the study of the twenty-six schools.

Table D-2. Comparison of School A and School B in Innovativeness

1. School Innovativeness — Professional Personnel

Variable	School A			School B		
	Mean Pre-	Mean Post-	Gain	Mean Pre-	Main Post-	Gain
Attitude	2.87	2.63	+ .23	2.70	2.38	+ .32
Availability	33.75	45.00	+11.25	35.33	38.25	+2.92
Usage	29.00	39.75	+10.75	38.33	36.50	-1.83

150

2. Student Participation in Innovative Endeavors

Variable	School A			School B		
	Mean Pre-	Mean Post-	Gain	Mean Pre	Main Post-	Gain
Classroom and Project Use						
Total	1.08	5.30	4.23	3.50	2.91	-0.65

Table D-3. School Professionals' Perception of Administrative Leadership and Communication to Community

	School A (N=28) Mean	School B (N=26) Mean	26 Schools Mean
Administrators' Leadership in Introducing Innovations	4.6	3.7	4.4
Faculty Attitude Toward Innovation	4.4	4.3	4.2

Table D-4. School Climate of Trust, Openness, and Adaptability (COPED)

	School A (N=28) Mean	School B (N=26) Mean
Trust	11.5	11.5
Openness	5.0	5.4
Adaptability	7.7	7.4

Table D-5. Board Member and Parent Characteristics and Attitudes*

Variable	School A (N=8) Mean	School B (N=5) Mean	Average for 26 Schools in Study
A. Board Members			
Economic Status (Income)	4.0	4 6	4.0
Own Attitude Toward Innovation	4.6	3.4	4.6
Attitude Toward Parental Pressure to Have School Innovate	3.8	3.8	3.7
Attitude Toward Board Pressuring School Administration to Innovate	4.6	3.4	4.2
Perception of Financial Resources for Innovation	3.0	3.4	2.5
Information about the Kettering Project	3.6	2.8	3.2

*Notes: 1. The averages are based on a five-point form, 1 (very low) to 5 (high or very much.)
2. A difference of approximately .4 between school means is needed for significance, at the .05 level.
3. Most of the information was gathered in the post-survey except for demographic information which was from pre-survey results.

151

Variable	School A (N=50) Mean	School B (N=11) Mean	Average for 26 Schools in Study
B. Parents			
Level of Personal Income	3.7	3.4	3.6
Community Acceptance of New	3.1	2.6	2.8
Attitude Toward Parental Pressure to have School Innovate	3.9	3.6	3.6

A COMPARISON OF TWO ACTION RESEARCH PROJECTS
(Alliance for Schools and League of Cooperating Schools)

Comparison of I/D/E/A/'s* *League of Cooperating Schools* in Southern California with the unfolding Alliance of Schools and Colgate University Program, reveals a number of interesting similarities and differences. In April 1971, one staff member of the Colgate Project and two participating area administrators observed the League for the purpose of comparing the two projects, providing possible further in-puts into the Alliance concept, and formulating guidelines for the planning of similar innovative projects. The resulting analysis concentrates on several high-order conceptual issues, such as institutionalization, the newly formed social system of participating schools, articulation between school and University, and peer intervention strategy.

The League of Cooperating Schools

The League, very briefly described, is a network of eighteen elementary and junior high schools located in the vicinity of Los Angeles, California. It was created by I/D/E/A (Institute for the Development of Educational Activities, Inc. an affiliate of the Charles F. Kettering Foundation) for the purpose of studying the process of educational change through action research. Schools were selected deliberately to represent a cross-section of American society and in no case is more than one school unit within a given district participating. Individual school units within districts were "borrowed" in League activities with an understanding that such participation might very well lead to changes which deviate from district norms. Two major ideas formed the basis for the original plan, both formulated by Goodlad of U.C.L.A.: (1) the individual school unit is the key unit of change in education — not the district, nor the individual classroom; and (2) the school principal is the key agent of change.

The actual innovations decided upon were left up to the discretion of the school staff. The institute has been interested in promoting a broad concept of change, not any specific innovation. Again, it is the individual school staff, led by the principal, which holds the key to change in the conceptual framework designed by I/D/E/A. The Institute's role has been to nurture change, help create the necessary environment for the institutionalization of reform, and to evaluate and report upon the processes observed.

The League, then can be thought of as a new unit of organization superimposed over existing relationships, with the existing relationships purposely weakened. The "new social system" developed its own pattern of roles, expectations and rewards in support of the change process with necessary linkages provided by frequent meetings, visitations by teachers, visits by staff, newsletters, and social events. Within the context of the "new social system" the concept of peer support took on new importance. The emotional and professional support usually missing when principals and staff venture alone on distinctly new paths could be provided by the teams of other innovating professionals in the League, even though spread over a wide geographic area.

Both the League and the Kettering-Colgate Project began with strong research orientation, and a commitment to encourage constructive and effective change in

---

*Institute for Development of Educational Activities, Inc., an affiliate of the Charles F. Kettering Foundation.

participating schools. In both cases the actual decisions as to the type of change introduced were a decision to be made primarily by the professionals within the schools, thus encouraging a rich diversity in types of innovations. However, several important differences in approach to change become evident from a comparison of the two projects. These include:

Institutionalization

The Kettering-Colgate Project, even before the crystallization of the notion of an Alliance of Schools and University, attempted to work through existing educational agencies. Planning sessions, funding proposals and implementation have been carried out with the intention of legitimization and continuance within established organizations (e.g., BOCES, Che-Mad-Her-On, School Boards, and Colgate University). Among the problems of this approach are those of coordination and conflicting interests. These have to be weighed against the benefits of institutionalized patterns of cooperation.

The League was designed, on the other hand, as a "new social system" (a system outside of the regular one) created by I/D/E/A and capable of exerting a strong countervailing force in the face of the resisting tendencies of existing systems. League principals are now discussing the need to continue at least the framework of the League if foundation support ends. This is a recognition on their part of the value of the relationship. The theory is that in any innovating school there are two groups: a small one composed of innovating teachers, and the larger one composed of other teachers and administrators. The smaller group views change as the norm. The larger group views the change as threatening. Usually the school board system of the school favors the large group, which means that innovative teachers' norms will be rejected and that the teachers may leave the system. The new League helps the innovating staff members resist the pressures to return to out-dated programs. But a real question raised here concerns the extent to which a completely "in-system" approach to change is necessary. Arguments used by advocates of such change models as the voucher system need not be recounted here to evidence the strong diversity in views on this issue. The Kettering-Colgate Project opted for a more "in-system" approach and while painfully aware of its short-comings, has been gratified by the initiative taken by several of the schools.

Perhaps two relatively recent influences have provided the conditions whereby the "in-system" has a greater chance of success than before. There is a trend for teacher associations to take more responsibility for developing programs in teacher preparation for improving their own school programs. This tends to raise the professional status of teachers by making them equals with university staff and other experts. The second, and related, influence may be teacher acceptance of the practice of looking beyond their own immediate group for new ideas and for evaluation (cosmopolitanism vs. provincialism). Both of these influences are decreasing the tendency of schools to perpetuate the status quo and this makes less necessary the creation of a "new social system" or out-group to provide the necessary peer support. Peer support could be provided if a group or council of innovating teachers were invited to volunteer and work, and given official sanction by the administration. The idea of peer-group strategy is nevertheless a very important concept and much needed.

The "bonus" for programs using the in-group approach is that planning help, financial support and healthy feedback and criticism are received from established social institutions such as school boards and regional and State planning agencies. For example, school board members and planning agencies may become favorably disposed toward the changes and thus provide strong psychological support to those involved in the project. If they are considered part of this in-group, they are informed and abreast of the changes. They then help provide moral and financial support.

Target Population

The Kettering-Colgate Project began working with individuals and small groups of teachers within project schools, with the approval, but usually not the continuing active participation, of administrators. As the project continued, selected departments and larger groups of professionals became actively involved, reflecting the "spreading" influence of the project as well as a growing awareness on the part of participants of the need for wider school participation if more meaningful changes were to take place in project schools. Restraints on such factors as scheduling, staff deployment and latitude of decision-making were sample key factors in pointing to the need for the broader approach. The Alliance, the most recent step taken, recognized more fully the need for the widest participation possible within any given system, including key administrators, to nurture the needed environment for change. In this way, the Kettering-Colgate Project has taken steps which more clearly resemble the original conception and processes of the League in each school. One of the observations that particularly impressed the representatives of the Kettering-Colgate Project while visiting League schools was the totality of the approach to change the building level, a factor not achieved to date in our project.

Articulation with a Teacher-Training Program

Teacher-Training Programs across the nation face a number of dilemmas, one of which is especially important to the staff at Colgate: how to develop teacher leaders, scholarly in their field and open to experimentation with change, indeed, initiating change, while recognizing the socialization potency and status quo orientation of the schools in which the prospective teachers carry out their internships. One of the goals of the Alliance is to associate teaching interns with changing educational environments, so they may become active participants and observers of the process. While many of the League schools have evolved certain relationships with teacher training institutions, a recent report indicates that provisions for prospective teachers is a problem still to be solved. Perhaps the internship aspect of the Alliance model may suggest a way that this may be done in future projects.

Peer Support

The concept of peer support took on new meaning in the League project. Innovators, especially those working in institutions known for their resistance to change, usually do not have the emotional or professional support from other participants in the institution. The League provided this needed peer support for change by creating linkages between innovating schools and professionals and by helping to create a social system with change and improvement being important characteristics built into role expectations. A question has to be raised as to the extent to which this desire to "open" the League participants to change resulted in "closing" the new social system to legitimate criticism and feedback from existing institutions. Did the League's stress on such concepts as autonomy and the idea of a "new social system" close the system to constructive outside criticism? The Kettering-Colgate Project did not try to isolate itself from regional and district boards of education and did not develop a social system among participating schools. Indeed, it often assisted other schools, not officially in the Project, to innovate.

During the first and second years, it did arrange group conferences at which innovating teachers made presentations and could associate and exchang ideas, so that some peer support was available. Many comments from the innovating teachers first associated with the project were directed toward the importance of the first summer workshops which brought the teachers into direct contact and communication. Linkages after that summer were mainly through consulting sessions with staff personnel and through newsletters, up until the time the project began working with whole departments. It is obvious that the Kettering-Colgate Project has not made full use of the "peer support" concept, which is no doubt helpful and needed. The importance of the concept of peer support to League participants and the emergence of the concept in the Kettering-Colgate Project, suggest that serious consideration be given it. It manifests itself concretely in such forms as frequent professional and social meetings by members, a variety of forms of communication and a number of linkages provided by project staff.

Whether the "new social system" must be made up of schools abstracted from their districts or whether the peer support effect could have been attained in the Kettering-Colgate Project model, if the need for it had been recognized, is a question that remains to be answered. The League model has uncovered an important concept which seems to go beyond the formation of a separatist cult.

COOPERATING PERSONNEL AND INSTITUTIONS (1968 – 71)
SCHOOL ADMINISTRATORS AND LIAISON PERSONNEL
Experimental Group

Bainbridge-Guilford High School
Bainbridge, New York
Mr. Thomas Braccio,
    Administrator and Liaison

Canastota Junior-Senior High School
Canastota, New York
Donald Rielle
Mr. Richard Evans, Administrator
    and Liaison

Cazenovia High School
Cazenovia, New York
Mr. William Haase, Administrator
Mr. Jesse Zeck, Liaison

Chadwicks Union Free
Chadwicks, New York
Mr. Joseph Jursak, Administrator
    and Liaison

Clinton Central School
Clinton, New York
Mr. Robert S. Grogan
Mr. Robert Ater, Administrator
Mr. Joseph Gee, Liaison

Cooperstown Central School
Cooperstown, New York
Mr. N.J. Sterling, Administrator
Mr. James Robinson, Liaison

Edmeston Central School
Edmeston, New York
Mr. Frank Mullet, Administrator
Mr. Alonzo DuMont, Liaison

Frankfort-Schuyler Central High School
Frankfort, New York
Mr. Andrew Mulligan
Mr. Anthony Borgognoni, Administrator
Mrs. Virginia Reina, Liaison

Greene Central School
Greene, New York
Mr. Robert Bennett, Administrator
Mr. Roland Wolford
Mr. Martin Felsen, Liaison

Hamilton Central School
Hamilton, New York
Mr. Gerald Douglass, Administrator
Mr. Harold Chapman, Liaison

Illion Junior-Senior High School
Illion, New York
Mr. James H. Dunn
Mr. Leo Sammon, Administrator
    and Liaison

Madison Central School
Madison, New York
Mr. William Rasbeck, Administrator
Mr. Michael Hayduk, Liaison

Milford Central School
Milford, New York
Mr. Gordon Hammond
Mr. Thomas Sheeran, Administrator
    and Liaison

Morrisville-Eaton Central School
Morrisville, New York 13408
Mr. Edward Andrews, Administrator
Mr. William O'Brien, Liaison

Mount Upton High School
Mount Upton, New York
Mr. Martin Maloney
Mr. Clifford McClean, Administrator
Mr. Ronald Kodra, Liaison

New York Mills High School
New York Mills, New York
Mr. William Quinn, Administrator
Mr. Richard Dunn, Liaison

Norwich Senior High School
Norwich, New York
Mr. Ivan Hunt, Administrator
Mr. Alex Swaab
Mr. Paul Preuss, Liaison

Oneida Senior High School
Oneida, New York
Mr. Edward T. Greene
Mr. Norman Burton, Administrator
Miss Norene Garlock, Liaison

Oriskany Falls High School
Oriskany Falls, New York
Mr. Walter Buckoski, Administrator
    and Liaison

Oxford Academy and Central High School
Oxford, New York
Mr. Richard Heller, Administrator
Mr. Lawrence Paser, Liaison

Rome Free Academy
Rome, New York
Mr. John F. MacDonald
Mr. Ralph Furiel, Administrator
Mr. Paul Delpiano, Liaison

Sauquoit Valley Central School
Sauquoit, New York
Dr. Theodore Soistmann, Administrator
Mr. William Moll, Liaison

Sherburne-Earlville Central School
Sherburne, New York
Mr. Richard A. Lagoe, Administrator
Mr. Joseph Martinelli, Liaison

Springfield Central School
East Springfield, New York
Mr. Robert Purple, Administrator
    and Liaison

Utica Free Academy
Utica, New York
Mr. Edward J. Perry
Mr. Anthony Schepsis, Administrator
Mr. Anthony Zane, Liaison

Van Hornesville Central School
Van Hornesville, New York
Mr. Robert Woodruff, Administrator
    and Liaison

Vernon-Verona-Sherrill High School
Verona, New York
Mr. Robert Williams, Administrator
Mrs. Elinoa Bellinger, Liaison

---

*NOTE: For names of innovating teachers see Appendix C.

SCHOOL ADMINISTRATORS AND LIAISON PERSONNEL
Control Group

Altona Central School
Altona, New York
Mr. Williams Slocum, Administrator
and Liaison

Beekmantown Central School
Plattsburgh, New York
Mr. Francis Ryan, Administrator
Mr. John Glasgow, Liaison

North Senior High School
Binghamton, New York
Mr. George Tate, Administrator
and Liaison

Deposit Central School
Deposit, New York
Dr. Michael Grenis, Administrator
Mr. Lawrence Bilow, Liaison

Dryden High School
Dryden, New York
Mr. William Deming, Administrator
Mr. Paul Volanti, Liaison

Elmira Free Academy
Elmira, New York
Mr. G.E. Bradley, Administrator
Mr. Henry Hughes, Liaison

Hadley-Luzerne Central School
Lake Luzerne, New York
Mr. Stuart Townsend, Administrator
and Liaison

Harpursville Central School
Harpursville, New York
Mr. Robert Spencer, Administrator
Mr. Franklin Cism, Liaison

Hartford Central School
Hartford, New York
Mr. George Snyder, Administrator
and Liaison

Union Springs High School
Union Springs, New York
Mr. John Baader, Administrator
Mr. Richard Moon, Liaison

West Canada Valley Central School
Newport, New York
Mr. Arthur Whaley, Administrator
Mr. George Metcalf, Liaison

Windsor Central School
Windsor, New York
Mr. Theron Philley, Administrator
Mr. Merritt Klumpp, Liaison

DEPARTMENT OF EDUCATION STAFF

Suzanne Brennan, Special Instructor in Methods, Mathematics

James Clarke, Associate Professor of Education and Social Sciences (Consultant)

Thomas Mendenhall, retired, Associate Professor of Education and Natural Sciences

E. Duane Meyer, Director of Field Services, Assistant Professor of Educational Administration

Eunice Gardner Palmer, retired, Special Instructor in Methods, Social Studies

Lawrence Przekop, Assistant Professor of Education and Natural Sciences

James Rankin, Assistant Professor of Education, Director of Intern Program

Linden Summers, Professor of Education (Consultant)

Donald S. Williams, Associate Professor of Education and English

Charles Hetherington, Professor of Education, Emeritus

(See also Kettering-Colgate Program Staff.)

BOCES

Conrad Rupert, District Superintendent of Schools for Madison-Oneida Counties Board of Cooperative Educational Services

Eugene Wieand, District Superintendent of Schools, Sole Supervisory District of Delaware, Chenango and Otsego Counties

CHE-MAD-HER-ON

Walter Lowerre, Director

George Purple, Associate Director

STATE EDUCATION DEPARTMENT

Michael Van Ryn, Director of In-Service Program

Norman Kurland, Director, Center on Innovation in Education

CONSULTANTS TO THE PROJECT

Herbert Walberg, Harvard University
(Consultant)

Frederick Fralick, Syracuse, New
York, Rater

Dorothy Judd Sickels, Editor of
final report

Richard Heller, Norwich, New York,
Rater

Peter P. Fay, Colgate University,
Senior Student

Raymond Ries, Professor of
Sociology, Colgate University

E. Howard Borck, Instructor in
Sociology, Colgate University

KETTERING–COLGATE STAFF

George E. Schlesser, Director

Robert Crowley, Assistant Director
of Research

David Jenkins, Media Specialist

Jennie Baumbach, Resource Teacher

William Moynihan, Resource Teacher

Donald Rudy, Resource Teacher

Patricia Doyle, Secretary to Project

Harriet Sprague, Computer
Programmer

(Other Early Planners Prior to the Operation of the Program – 1967)

Gene Moser, University of Pittsburgh   Lawrence Ulin, Gallup-Robinson, Inc.

John Beyer, Colgate University

COLGATE UNIVERSITY ADMINISTRATION

Thomas A. Bartlett,
President

Franklin W. Wallin, Dean
of the Faculty

INDEX

Administrative leadership, 47
  openness, trust and
    adaptability, 47-48
  power and authority, 58-61

Alliance of schools, 12
  comparison with League of
    schools, 153-156
  definition of, 12
  major features, 12-18
  pilot program, 12-13
  plan, summary 13-14
  teacher preparation in, 19-22

Articulation,
  joint utilization of staffs, 21
  interchange of students, 22

Attitude toward innovation
  change and stability in, 77
  definition of, 30
  instrument for measuring, 77-79
  relative importance of forces
    related to, 63-64
  validity and reliability of
    measure, 77

Availability of innovations
  definition of, 30-31
  instrument, 81-86
  relative importance of forces
    related to, 63-64
  stability and change in, 77
  validity and reliability
    of instrument, 80

Bachman, J. G., 61

Board members' power, 37-42
  attitudes and actions related to
    criteria, 41-42

Board of Cooperative Educational
  Services cooperation with
    Kettering-Colgate Project, 16
  place in organizational
    structure, 17
  purpose of, 16

Borck, E. Howard, 58

Brickell, H. M., 34, 37, 43

Brochures
  communicative power, 52-53
  influence of, 51-52
  on professional staff, 53

Buckmiller, Archie, 145

Campbell, Donald T., 33, 148

Carlson, R. O., 41

Change
  attitude toward rapidity of, 44, 46
  definition and measurement
    of, 147-149
  regression and measurement
    of change, 147-148

Colgate University
  changes in teacher-preparation,
    21-23
  influence of Project on, 19

Community forces, 34
  instrument for measuring, 88-92
  reliability of instrument, 87
  relation to school innovativeness,
    (see Forces)

Correlation coefficient
  meaning of, 26

Criteria (attitude, availability and usage)
  definitions of, 30-31

Crowley, Robert J., 145

Curriculum Research Center, 19

Decision-making pattern, 58

Departmental Units
  development of, 7-10
  planning and summary, 9, 13
  schools participating in, 7

Diffusion, 110-141
  by innovating teacher, 25-26
  evaluation form, innovational
    experience, 28
  effectiveness of training
    program, 26
  related to criteria, 25-27
  school awareness of, 26-27

Doll, Ronald C., 43

Dubois, Philip, 145

Dynamics of Innovation in two
  schools
  board member characteristics
    in, 151
  innovativeness, 150
  leadership and morale, 58-61

Educational lag, 68-69

Experimental-control groups,
  relative gains on criteria, 72-75

162